"Who would have ever thought that rock would become such an important venue for debates about religion in our culture? In *Rock Stars On God*, Doug Van Pelt shows us that rock stars are engaged in discussing life's big issues as never before." —Mark Joseph, author, *Faith, God & Rock 'n' Roll*

"'What So & So Says' is one of the most interesting features in any music magazine. Doug Van Pelt gives you a spiritual look into artists' lives that uninspired journalists would be afraid to approach intelligently." —Tim M. Cook, Cook Management, P.O.D., Blindside

"One thing I always admired about Doug Van Pelt's interviews for *HM* magazine is that he never misquotes the artist he is interviewing. In an age where sensationalism overrides honesty, it is refreshing to hear what the artist really has to say in the whole context. Because of this one aspect, I have much respect! May this book not fall on deaf ears." —Doug Pinnick, King's X

"Once again, Doug asks all the right questions and pushes all the right buttons. This is a fascinating look into the spiritual lives of those whom we idolize and emulate." —Bob Beeman, Pastor Sanctuary International

"For years *HM* magazine has served up thoughtful interviews with various mainstream rock artists, getting a handle on their thoughts about life, the world, their particular 'take' on music, and their own lyrics—as well as spirituality and issues regarding Jesus and the Good News. I've read and loved 'em from the first. What a great idea to publish them in book form! You'll find yourself liking some, shuddering at others, but always thinking and hopefully praying as a result." —Glenn Kaiser, pastor and musician

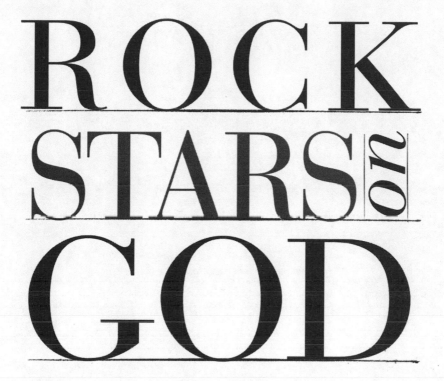

ROCK STARS on GOD

ROCK STARS on GOD

BY DOUG VAN PELT

{ [RELEVANTBOOKS] }

Published by Relevant Books
A division of Relevant Media Group, Inc.

www.relevantbooks.com
www.relevantmediagroup.com

Design: Relevant Solutions
www.relevant-solutions.com
Cover design: Mark Arnold
Interior design: Jeremy Kennedy

For information or bulk orders:
RELEVANT MEDIA GROUP, INC.
POST OFFICE BOX 951127
LAKE MARY, FL 32795
407-333-7152

Library of Congress Control Number: 2004090401
International Standard Book Number: 0-9729276-9-7

04 05 06 07 9 8 7 6 5 4 3 2 1

Printed in the United States of America

THANKS:

My wife, Charlotta Van Pelt, who believes in the vision of *HM* magazine and this book; my two lovely daughters, Kaela and Rachel, who love me unconditionally; my parents, Larry and Carolyn Van Pelt, for buying me my first computer, and getting *Heaven's Metal* into the computer age; all the publicists who helped set up these interviews (too numerous to mention: Michael Mazur, Steve Karas, Glenn Fukushima, Rhonda Saenz, Stephanie Kavoulakos, Tracy Zamot, Sophie Diamantis, Chip Ruggieri, Jeff Sipler, Mark Morton, Rick Orienza, Heather Davis, Anna Adame, Terry Wang, Bill Metoyer, Bryn Bridenthal, to name a few); all the artists interviewed, for their time and conversation; and all the *HM* readers through the years who kept encouraging me to publish this as a book.

Unless otherwise noted, each of these interviews was conducted by the author, Doug Van Pelt. Other interviewers included are: Phil Chalmers, Kevin Bullard, David Jenison, Eric Shirey, Jamie Lee Rake, Katrina "aka Gordon" Johns, David M. Pogge, Jason E. Dodd, and Ginny McCabe.

This book would not have been possible had it not been for the help in transcribing. Doing an interview takes several steps. First, you've got to come up with questions. Sometimes this requires putting yourself in the mind of your readers and your interview subject. After going through the logistics of setting up the interview, you've next got to record the actual interview. If it's a face-to-face interview, you either hold the micro-cassette recorder, set it down on a nearby surface, or ask the subject to hold it. If it's over the telephone, you need to have one of the low-budget James Bond conversation recorder devices. After the interview's over, you've got to sit down and transcribe it. This involves playing the tape back, pausing the tape while writing down what you hear, and then playing some more. Having a transcriber machine with a foot pedal to pause the action helps, but it takes a strong willingness to plow through a twenty, thirty, forty-five minute, or an hour conversation. Many thanks go out to the myriad of individuals who have done this for *HM* over the past years: Andy Crump, Camille Bresie, Brian McGovern, Ben Mengden, David DeStefano, Kim Philpott, Lorna Hunt, Michelle Pierce, Wilco DeLange, Amanda Nelson, Katrina Johns, Tim McCready, Rick Koch, Jason Dodd, Brian Rutherford, Bethany Read, Sarah Day, Bonnie Plott, Jonathan Nolte, Valerie Allen, Daniel Markham, Jeffrey Ellinger, Justin Dewberry, and Christopher Rose. You all know what it takes! Thank you.

TABLE OF CONTENTS

FOREWORD

by Michael Sweet, in collaboration with Dave Rose of Deep South Entertainment

Have you ever wanted to have a personal and intimate conversation with a rock star about their beliefs? My great friend of many years, Doug Van Pelt, does just that, almost every day. And now he's sharing these conversations with you. Over the years, Doug has consistently provided "behind the scenes" style interviews with some of rock music's most notable people, discussing a vast array of topics, including ones most journalists don't dare tackle.

How do you feel about Jesus Christ? What is your philosophy of life? If you die today, what happens? No matter what you believe, wouldn't it be engaging to have a "hidden camera" look into how famous rock stars feel on these subjects? No matter what your spiritual beliefs are, or what your religious background is, Doug Van Pelt provides some eye-opening responses to some of the most personal subject matters, directed toward some of rock music's most notable names: Kiss, Metallica, Henry Rollins, Alice Cooper, Sammy Hagar, Nickelback, and Godsmack, just to name a few.

Through his interviews, Doug has always been able to bring out the best in people. He gets them to explore areas, topics, and thoughts that are often uncharted waters in the world of rock star interviews. People open up to Doug, as displayed in these pages. From topics about music to religion, touring to accountability, Doug has intimate discussions about even the most sacred and personal subjects.

Being in Stryper, I have been interviewed over the years by thousands and have been asked almost every question under the sun. Stryper has always been up front with our beliefs. We are a Christian band, so questions about God, religion, and spirituality were not only expected, but welcomed. This is not necessarily the case, though, with most rock bands. Most rock bands can live out their entire career and possibly never get asked about Jesus Christ or their spiritual beliefs. Doug has changed all this.

Doug Van Pelt has brought rock star interviews to a new level. Interviews with Doug, as I have personally experienced, aren't interviews at all. They are more like two friends sitting down over a cup of coffee. They are conversations, not interviews. He articulates these conversations with integrity, personality, and general interest in getting to know the "real person" behind the rock star.

Music is one of the most powerful mediums in the world. If affects people's emotions. It can bring joy or sadness. It can motivate or depress. Music is one of the most potent and influential forms of expression known to mankind. I have personally witnessed the power of music my entire life. Doug's honest and candid (some may say tenacious) approach to journalism has always managed to highlight this reality and how it relates spiritually.

Doug Van Pelt and I basically grew together in the music business, as we both got our start around the same time. I first met Doug in early 1985 when Stryper was touring through Texas. We were playing at the Austin opera house. Doug took Oz [Fox] and I down Guadeloupe Street there in Austin to a clothing store that was selling some yellow and black clothes. This was the beginning of a long and uplifting friendship between the two of us.

His first issue of *Heaven's Metal* (as it was called then) came out in June of 1985 and featured Stryper on the cover. He has been a regular writer for *CCM* as well as *Guitar World* magazines and continues to publish *HM* magazine. Above all, he has been the consistent leader in the industry for joining the topics of music and

God through printed medium. While his interviews and articles have not been entirely exempt from the ire of the Christian music community, Doug Van Pelt has remained true to his view that people do want to talk about and read about spiritual beliefs as they relate to rock music.

He has always delivered writings that were relevant, insightful, and often monumental to the music community, *Rock Stars on God* being a partial, but incredible, collection of some of these writings.

Thank you, Doug, for all that you have done to revolutionize music journalism and bring a fresh perspective to the wonderful gift of music.

INTRODUCTION

What you are reading is whole or complete excerpts from the pages of *HM* magazine (plus some unused interviews that have not, until this printing, seen the ink of a printed page). These interviews are word-for-word accounts or transcriptions from the actual conversations that took place, most often a recorded telephone interview. Each interview subject was being interviewed to promote his or her band's latest album. The interviews are captured here in their raw form, with almost all the "uhs," and "likes" and "you know what I means" that took place in the actual conversations (we took out a few just to keep it from being annoying!). The transcriptions stay true to the timing of the interviews as well, with no editing or "cut and pasting" of any quotes in one section so as to alter the true recording of the conversation as it took place.

Therefore, this is an unusual book. It is more a collection of interviews, like a collection of essays or daily devotionals. The reader can read a chapter casually and pick up the book later to read another and not miss a plot or theme. While I bring my own faith into the book, I do not assume the reader shares in this faith. The reader of this book gets the unusual perspective of being a witness, or "fly on the wall," on a conversation that reaches its crux with a discussion about the person of Jesus Christ. No matter which side of the fence the reader's allegiance falls on, "listening in" to a conversation about this specific historical figure always proves to be curiously intriguing and engaging. Much like in real life, the observer can say to him or herself (in the same way that this writer/interviewer does), "I would have said this," or "Oooh, I wish I could have remembered to bring *this* up."

While not many people would volunteer for the position of debater on things of Christ, I have found that people will enter into this debate if done so graciously and with tact.

[Note: The rest of this introduction is somewhat unusual in that it is almost "family business" or "insider's talk" about Christianity, evangelism, conversion, and how these subjects relate to this book. People who aren't Christians may read the following paragraphs and feel like they are "listening in" as their Christian relatives are in the next room talking about how to convince them to believe in God. While this may be a tad awkward (and you may want to skip ahead to the interviews), it will hopefully reveal a much less threatening of a mindset and strip away the misconception that non-believers are "spiritual projects" for believers or "notches on their Bible belts." A "conversion or nothing" agenda is obviously shallow and leads to a subtle attitude for believers of using people as objects, rather than valuing them as people. The interviews in this book are not examples of such an agenda. Instead, they are simple conversations or interviews that may or may not engage the reader's mind on the subject of spiritual things. This is certainly much less threatening than a Christian knocking on a person's door and confronting them about their eternal destiny. However, because this book is likely to be read by many believers, there may be reason to explain why the approach I've used in discussing God with rock stars was chosen. Thus, the following paragraphs are somewhat exclusive in thought.

One of the goals I have when I conduct the interviews for each "So & So Says" feature in *HM* is to establish a relationship. I am a firm believer in what has been termed "friendship evangelism," in other words, someone coming to faith in Christ through the influence of a friend. Street corner preaching and "cold call" evangelism with strangers is valid, and I've done both, but quite often a person's trust must be built up in order for them to actually hear what is being said. While keeping an open and obedient heart to the Holy Spirit's leading, I plan on and hope to be a part of the patient, long-term "harvesting" that happens to an individual when they place their trust and faith in Christ. This is a work of God in which I believe He gives us the privilege of participating, almost as just witnesses. If that never happens, though, then at least I've made a friend, and friendships are one of the best things about life on this earth in the first place.

It is often a friend or associate who leads a person to Christ, or who has the privilege of praying with a person to acknowledge their need of a Savior and making that miraculous transaction we call "salvation." With this in mind, I make it my goal to first establish a relationship with the interviewee or interview subject. I treat them with kindness and extend respect and dignity. This person is not a "project" of mine, but as long as talking about spiritual things comes up, the possibility of eternal things transpiring at least shines a special light on this "relationship," however brief it may be. I often inquire about meeting them in person (as often these interviews are conducted over the phone), with the goal of perhaps meeting them for a chat before or after a concert in the Austin area where I live. If this happens, as it occasionally does, then the interview subject has an opportunity to see and interact with a real-live Christian. This may sound funny, but often a resident of this modern world has never had personal interaction with a devout believer. Quite often a non-believer's viewpoint or perception of Christianity is based upon their observation of a television evangelist or a person picketing at one of their shows. Just to have interaction with a Christian who is normal and down-to-earth quite often disarms that negative stereotype of what a Christian is. If nothing else is accomplished but this false perspective being shattered, that is a good thing.

So, if one of my goals is this so-called "friendship evangelism," or if I'm able to influence this other person in any way, then honesty, humility, and trust are key factors. I hope to build up trust in my interview time. I do this by listening, and asking intelligent questions and follow-up questions that show I'm listening. When I "argue" or enter into debate with the interview subject on a certain issue or point, I try to do so in a non-offensive, unassuming way. I strategically use words and phrases that do not invite defensive reactions. For example, instead of stating that Jesus is trustworthy and that the New Testament is a reliable document, I'll state that *"I believe* Jesus is trustworthy," or that *"I believe* the New Testament to be a reliable document." Just to preface my statements with the words "I believe" disarms a defensive and reactionary response. It's a non-dogmatic approach that invites discourse, not a fight.

I know the interview subject will interact with me on a number of levels and, Lord willing, be confronted with the good news of Jesus Christ in one or all of these moments. The first interaction is the interview itself. Often the interview subject is either at a record company's offices or at their home, conducting several thirty-minute interviews back-to-back via phone. As is often the case, these artists are hearing the same or similar questions over and over again. It takes an effort to come up with original questions, which I try to do, but it almost comes completely as surprise and out of left field when I pose the question, "What do you think of Jesus Christ?" Most often the interviewee asks me to repeat the question, or they themselves repeat the question, as if to ask, "Are you *really* asking me this?" This is the first time they are confronted with the good news within the context of *HM* magazine. The second interaction is either meeting me at a show on the tour (which often takes place not too long after the interview is conducted and before the issue with their interview is even printed), or actually reading the printed interview. It's quite an interesting experience to be interviewed and to see your words in print at a later time. I've been on both sides of the interview process, so I know that it's often very interesting to read what you had to say in an interview that happened a few or several months prior. As might be the case with this book, the interviewee might be reading this a good ten years after the original conversation/interview. Oftentimes, this exposure to "the Jesus question" can hit them harder when reading this question and their response to it than the first time they were asked the question. It will sometimes make the interview subject ask themselves the question again.

The personal meeting at a show is often a low-key event, where they get to meet the person who interviewed them (which they may not even remember doing, unless I bring it up, as an artist often does several dozen interviews during a "press time" period that surrounds a new album release). This allows them to see that someone who is willing to ask them about Jesus Christ isn't a complete lunatic who has no basis or grounding in reality. Just interacting with them in a real, human way can often add more trust and respect to a growing relationship that could turn into friendship.

One thing I often do when interacting with famous people is to treat them like real people. I ask about their family. I interact with them in a conversational way. I don't preach or talk down to them or come to them in a "fan mentality," that just looks up to them and is impressed with their fame and talent. While adoration can be encouraging to an artist, it does not invite real interaction and relationship. Not many people will desire to interact with someone who adores them in such a way. Celebrities face this challenge on a daily basis. Who in their world can they trust or interact with? Who is being friendly to them in a genuine way, and who is being friendly to "get something" or use them? Keeping the conversation clear of the artist's status or fame is a way to let them know that you're not impressed with their fame, that you can relate to them as a real person, and that you can be trusted to interact with them in a pleasant way. If this interaction goes well, sometimes a friendship develops. I have been able to interact with some of my "So & So Says" interview subjects in this way. In the course of conversation, we tell the other person that, "I'd like to keep in touch," or "I'll see you, perhaps, next time you come through Austin." I've seen this happen with members of Brother Cane and Extreme, both of which featured singers who believe in Christ (and both of whom, ironically, went on to sing for other, bigger bands—Gary Cherone with Van Halen, and Damon Johnson with Damn Yankees). Sometimes the repeat interaction takes place simply due to another album coming out years later and another interview taking place. I've had a chance to speak to (Megadeth's) Dave Mustaine twice in this manner, once over the phone and once at a show, where I had the chance to talk to him afterward and hand him a copy of the magazine in which our interview was published.

The publishing of this book will afford more of these interactions to take place. Many of these artists will, perhaps, read the book due to our efforts to get one in their hands or simply see it in stores or advertised and simply "want to see what they said" (or check to see if they were quoted accurate-ly!).

I honestly do not wish for this introduction to simply act as defensive justification to paint these interviews as somehow being more spiritual than they are, or to defend this as "my ministry." I have, on rare occasion, heard criticism that I "back down" or "let these artists off too easy" in not consis-tently providing an airtight case in regards to the defense of the Gospel. Perhaps that is why I've gone out of my way to explain why these interviews are not fights or examples of "in-your-face-ism." Whenever someone does anything remotely spiritual in a public forum, they will undergo scrutiny and criticism. If my reasons for not "leading the interview subject in the 'sinner's prayer'" are not adequate enough, I will simply sigh and state that, "Hey, they're just interviews for a music magazine."

While I do not have the time or inclination to befriend and maintain close relationships with all of the more than ninety different artists I've inter- viewed in this manner, I truly believe what the Bible says about man's condition and his ultimate destination apart from the forgiveness and salvation offered by Jesus the Christ. And, if I truly believe this, then it is truly a goal of mine to try to lead anyone I talk to about spiritual things in the direction of Christ. I don't expect to convert an artist to Christ over the phone, but I hope I can be a part of the process that helps a person open their spiritual eyes to their need and their Savior. I've never asked an interview subject during an interview if they'd like to pray with me to receive Christ, nor do I expect that to happen, but I'm certainly open to the idea if the Holy Spirit leads me in that direction. An approach like that would be, in my terms, "short-term evangelism," as opposed to what I'm talking about—"long-term evangelism." My commission in Scripture (Matthew 28:18-20), accepted as a "fellow" disciple of Christ, is carried out in many ways. This book and these interviews, while not clearly under the obligation to show fruit toward the "Great Commission," is surely bearing long-term fruit in the lives of many readers. Hopefully, some believing readers will be encouraged to spark up more conversations on spiritual matters and do so boldly and without reservation, and some non-believing readers will be challenged to re-think their resistance to the greatest news ever brought to mankind.

One of my goals for this column in my magazine was articulated for me by the producer of the first four King's X albums on Megaforce and Atlantic Records (as well as directing the "TV Dinners" video by ZZ Top)—Sam Taylor. Sam thanked me for printing the exact words that members of "his bands" had spoken during my interviews. It is commonplace for journalists to either take notes on a notepad during an interview, or transcribe only portions of a recorded interview. Often what an artist says in an interview is paraphrased and, all too commonly, misquoted. Sam thanked me for not misquoting "his artists," and went on to encourage me to keep this up with the "So & So Says" features. He said that one day artists would fight among themselves as to which member could do the interview for *HM* magazine, that our reputation would grow favorably as people found out it was a forum in which they would be quoted accurately. Upon hearing this, I immediately began to make it one of my goals. I want the "So & So Says" features to be a highlight, not only for the reader of the magazine, but also for the artists being interviewed. It would make me very pleased to know that the members of some band like Megadeth were bickering over which one of them had the positive privilege of doing the interview for *HM* magazine. If we accomplish this, then I think we have accomplished what would satisfy true journalistic integrity, as well as simple integrity before a holy God.

Another unspoken goal of these interviews has been to simply be an enjoyable read and something *HM* readers will appreciate seeing in each issue. I think, by the grace of God, this goal has been accomplished. We have received many letters from readers over the years, telling us it is their favorite section of the magazine and/or the part they read first. We've also received our fair share of "Please interview this band," or "Please interview that band." One such enthusiastic reader suggested we interview the members of the '70s supergroup Boston. He even went so far as to supply me with the home phone numbers of vocalist Brad Delp and guitarist Tom Scholz! (I've yet to call them.) Because this section of the magazine has become so popular, it only seemed natural to collect as many of the features as possible and publish them as a book. What you are holding is a small collection of these interviews. Perhaps this collection will do well and warrant subsequent volumes that feature the rest of our collection of nearly one hundred interviews.

"Religion is so tied
up with political
manipulation
that it is hard
to see if there
could be a nugget
of spirituality in
there that can
genuinely influence
your life."

—Tom Morello

For most of 1993, when this interview occurred, Rage Against the Machine's *controversial debut album had been kept underground because of its radical, lyrical content; however, Rage's incredible music and stage show overcame the restraints as the group received major airplay in addition to being a part of that summer's giant Lollapalooza tour. In an interview with* HM *writer David Jenison, Rage Against the Machine guitarist Tom Morello spoke openly about the controversial message and ideas of one of America's hottest bands.*

First of all, I heard that you graduated from Harvard with honors. Would you tell me something more about this?

TM: "I majored in social studies, a subject which most people have not heard of since the fifth grade when they colored in maps. That was Harvard, but at $18,000 a year. I have mixed feelings about Harvard, because, on the one hand, I had great professors who really helped me to intellectually arm myself against the machine. On the other hand, it is a training ground for the next generation of the ruling elite and all that entails, from investments in companies, to business with South Africa, to the overall Kennedy school of (expletive)."

I am also interested in knowing more about your parents, because I heard that they are not the normal kind of parents. Would you mind telling me about them?

TM: "My father was a part of the Mau insurrection which freed Kenya from British colonial rule, and his uncle was the leader of the insurrection and became Kenya's first president. It was all a part of Africa's anti-colonial wave. However, Kenya is really having problems now.

"The times most worth living are the times of change and revolt. These are the times when right and wrong are most clear, purpose is most well-defined, and a person can judge his worth by how he carries out the courage of his conviction. However, once a person takes power, it becomes a whole different deal. Kenya is stuck in the bureaucratic melange where many of the former revolutionaries are now in big government jobs and have become more susceptible to the ply of the International Monetary Fund, and people like that who want to ensure Kenya stays firm in the capitalistic camp. The people who lose at the end of the day, now, are the Mau ground soldiers and their families who worked to liberate the country."

Would you tell me about your mom?

TM: "My mom is really radical. She founded and organized Parents For Rock and Rap, which battles the PMRC (Parents' Music Resource Center) at every legislative and record store turn. Whenever another ugly senator's wife's head raises, Parents For Rock and Rap will be there to shout it down. The organization really helps keep in the public's mind that not all 'adults' are opposed to rock music."

How do you feel about censorship?

TM: "Censorship is generally a smoke screen covering up the racial content of the matter. The latest wave of censorship height began when artists like Public Enemy and Ice-T became popular in the white suburbs. Though these artists were already selling a million records at a time in urban centers, when the music entered the white communities and Bon Jovi posters started coming down and Chuck D posters started going up in the bedrooms of white teenagers, the music became more threatening.

"If there was any real genuine concern for the well-being of young American boys and girls, then the censorship people would concentrate first on parental abuse and neglect, which is a truly debilitating affliction of our society, as opposed to rock lyrics. I long for the day when, right here, I will clear the desk, that someone will give me the first scientific study that shows that any rock lyric has ever adversely affected the behavior of any individual at any time. However, parental abuse and neglect has already been established as debilitating. Society does not want to recognize the real issues like abuse, AIDS, and homelessness among teenagers. It is easier to make bands like N.W.A. and Ice-T the scapegoats. However, some kids have more to fear from their parents or guardians than they do from any Ice Cube, Easy-E, or James Hetfield.

"Censorship is a distracting issue with which we should not even have to worry. Near the community in which I grew up in Northern Illinois, seventeen-year-olds cannot legally buy the Rage Against the Machine record. I wonder how much of it has to do with the people in power not wanting the virginal ears of seventeen-year-olds to hear the word (expletive) and how much they do not want them to hear, 'Landlords and power whores on my people they took turns,' which is far more dangerous of a statement."

Define "the machine."

TM: "The machine can be anything from the localized brutality of the domestic oppressive wing of the government, which is the police force, which harasses and intimidates the poor and minority communities, to the overall corporate capitalistic machine which has been running on the sweat and blood of the under classes for five hundred years and dehumanizes people by making them a willing and complacent cog. It is you and me raging against all that."

What is one of the most significant issues which the band opposes?

TM: "One of the most important issues to confront is the conservative propaganda of the educational system and the media which acts as its veil. In a hardcore dictatorship, the dictator says this is what you are going to do, and you do it, or you will be shot dead by the army. In America, there is not a hardcore dictatorship, but a soft one. In the upper elite, there are people, whether they are the captains of industry, the military, or the government, who make decisions and then sell them to the American people. They do not have to sell them to everybody, just to the 20 percent of the population who have their hands on the wheel, like the educated, people in management, university professors, and people who are soaked and indoctrinated in the official party line. The other 80 percent are people who have to be kept from thinking that they are without a job and eating out of a garbage can, or that they are in an employment which is not fulfilling in any way while the boss man reaps the profits of the physical labor they do. Their minds are kept busy thinking about other things like sports, game shows, and the lottery.

"I do not believe that it is an accident that in the educational system, history is taught as a set of dates in the past with no connection to where we are or what we are doing now. If people realized that history was not a set of stuffy dates set in the past, but a constantly evolving, conflicting recreation of the society in which they live, then they would see that they are active players in creating the future. A person is an active player whether he sits on his couch watching TV, advocating and keeping himself completely out of the realm of discourse, or if he is in the streets of Central America. Everyone contributes to what tomorrow will be. The purpose of everything—Miller Lite, Los Angeles Dodgers, *Love Connection*, the Lottery, and all that other (expletive) is to keep people's minds elsewhere so that we will merely sit there and let other people make the decisions. As our vocalist Zack so eloquently puts it, they are victims of the 'In House Drive By.'"

What is a social issue that is important to the group?

TM: "Homelessness is a great travesty. The last show we did in L.A. was a benefit for the L.A. poverty department, which provides not only shelter, but also a stage and gallery for people on skid row to read their poetry and display their artwork. People tend to forget that the homeless are people too. People see them as these shadowy figures that persuade them to lock their doors as they drive through downtown L.A. In the rock community, there is a sympathy for the homeless, but no recognition that they are people with artistic needs as well. The fact that our government is willing to spend billions of dollars on idiotic weapons systems, while, during the Reagan administration, we threw mentally handicapped people on the streets by the tens of thousands with no means to support themselves, is unconscionable and needs to be addressed. We can help the symptoms by doing benefits and charity, but the problem is a system which creates homelessness, not the fact that homelessness exists. We need to attack the problem at its root."

I know Rage performed in a pro-choice benefit concert a few months back called Rock for Choice with groups like the Screaming Trees, Stone Temple Pilots, Mary's Danish, and Pearl Jam's Eddie Vetter. How do you feel about the abortion issue?

TM: "An abortion should be a very difficult choice and should never be taken lightly, but the choice should not be made by the government. The government should not be able to legislate that a person has to make a particular decision. When the government gets involved in the issue, horrible things happen. During the Bush administration, there was some kind of statute saying something like a person must have both parents' consent to get an abortion if she was under eighteen. It was a complete denial that often a principle adversary in a young person's life is his or her parents. The desire for family values and to cleanse the way fails to acknowledge that there are real risks. Imagine the number of suicides that were prompted by that little bit of legislation. Bottom line, the government needs to stay out of a woman's womb."

What do you think about religion, Christianity in particular?

TM: "I was raised Catholic, and went to a Catholic school for a year, and it was at Catholic school that I had my first problem. My mom realized I was being treated differently because of the color of my skin. I do not believe that racism was a Christian tenant being prescribed, but it was something which the positive ideology of Catholicism had no power over. You cannot control a racist nun. My family is Italian Roman Catholic and goes to church every single day, and I think there can be an empowering aspect to religion. In Liberation Theology, for example, the desire to affect social change and matters here on earth for the better, whether it be bringing down tyrants or helping people who have nothing, has proven to be an empowering instrument. Given the right spin, religion can be helpful. Otherwise, completely regardless of any sort of celestial beings, religion is used as a political tool on this earth by those who are in power to keep people who are not in power powerless. Regardless of what really happened two thousand years ago in Bethlehem, that is the reality of religion's social manifestation today."

I agree with you that the majority of churches are stuck in power struggles and social manipulation—how you would suggest they should be changed?

TM: "I can honestly say that no one has ever asked me that question before. In Catholicism especially, the people are deeply locked in tradition and doctrines. For example, they cannot have women priests or use contraceptives. It is alright if there are starving babies, but a person cannot put latex on his penis. Every so often, though, they do back off on something. For example, they said, 'Okay, the pope is not infallible.' We say, 'Good. We knew that, but now we are glad you do too. Progress.'

"On the other hand, people have found inspiration to confront tyrants from Christian doctrine. My aunt and uncle are deeply religious, which gives them a peace of mind they might not otherwise have."

Outside of the corruption of the Church, what do you believe about God, if you do believe in Him?

TM: "I do not know. My concentration has always been on throwing people against the wall who use our tax money to finance death squads. Those are the issues which occupy my head, and not religion.

"In the town in which I lived as a youth, religion was king. In fact, rock religion was king. I mean, Libertyville, Illinois, must have been the Christian rock capital of the Midwest. I was so surprised when I came out to Southern California and there were no Christian rock bands."

Actually, there are a large number of Christian rock bands in California.

TM: "Really? They must not have the same profile. Well, in the ad sections of the music newspapers, a third of them were asking for a Christian musician. The ads would say something like, 'Wanted: A Christian bassist.' Well, I am an agnostic bassist, but they would say, 'You will not do. We will be needing a Christian bassist for this band.' There was a real intolerance with Christianity against outsiders.

"This is a little known fact, but I used to go to a church youth group. I did not go for the religious aspect, but because they would say, 'Let's keep kids off drugs,' and then we would go play all these games. I had a great time going, and the people were really nice. However, I never went again after this one time. It was around Christmas time, and the climax of the service was singing a song about how happy they were that it was Christmas, while the song dissed every other world religion in sarcastic terms, like, 'Aren't those people stupid!' There was no respect or tolerance for other people's beliefs. Even if a person is so vain as to believe the religion he was indoctrinated into is the one true religion, what about the person who was born in Hindu India?

"When I first went to Harvard, there was a guy who was always attempting to convert me. We always had great theological discussions. We would argue continuously. He was always stuck on the point, 'If you do not accept Jesus Christ as your Savior, you are just going to go to hell.' That is just so unfair, because what about the kid who has never heard those two words put together—Jesus Christ? The kid grew up a Buddhist, and he never heard about Jesus. My friend responded by telling me some story from the Bible about a guy going down a road and an angel came down and said something. Some story about a guy who knew nothing about God and was converted through divine intervention. You and I both know that in Bangladesh there are not like a billion angels descending right now, and that all these people who may be good, bad, or indifferent, just like you or me, are all going to be cast into hell because they were cursed with being that semen and that egg that got together in the Sub-continent of Africa. They will spend eternal life in misery merely because they were born in the wrong continent."

I am interested to hear what you would say about the person who has heard the name Jesus Christ. What do you think will happen if he does believe?

TM: "I do not know. Maybe I would have a more positive view of religion if I was impressed by the behavior of those who preach it, not meaning preachers, but anyone, from the heads of government to the people I know in the school who confessed to be Christians. Some of those Christians were the biggest (expletive) who mistreated their fellow man in the worst ways. Religion is so tied up with political manipulation that it is hard to see if there could be a nugget of spirituality in there that can genuinely influence your life. It is hard to find. Zack, our vocalist, is more into spirituality. He draws on examples of Martin Luther King and Malcolm X, two deeply religious people, whom he claims would never have been able to translate their radical philosophies in as powerful a way if it were not for their deep religious convictions and spirituality, which was linked with their belief in their different gods. Without their beliefs, they would not have been able to communicate with the same kind of passion, which is what made them important. However, I counter Zack by saying, 'While they were both very important communicators, we still live in a racist, capitalistic society despite their efforts, because neither of them realized that the principle problems we have here are class based and not based on race or religion.'"

I know I only have time for one more question, so I must ask you about the incredible guitar sounds you make. How do you get your sounds?

TM: "Look at this, at the end of the interview, you finally ask me a music question! Well, I do not have the rack gear because it is expensive, hard to understand, and tends to make all guitarists sound the same. I have four grimy effects pedals, and I use them to the best of my ability. I am really embarrassed when people compliment me on my guitar playing because I think I am a terribly mediocre, undisciplined guitarist. If my playing has anything going for it, it is that I have a bit of imagination, which is very rare. 'Guitarists need to look beyond the norm of guitar playing.' Everyone says that if you like these certain groups and guitarists. When people get out of that thinking mode, they can just make noises with it. I do not feel I make the noises as good as I could, or as good as some creative genius like Jimi Hendrix or Jimmy Page could have done if they had stumbled upon the same kind of sounds I did. I merely got beyond the tunnel vision. The guitar sounds I make are easy to play. It is inspiration more than technical ability. Much of the inspiration comes from sitting around, and rather than playing with a pick, playing with a wrench and seeing how it sounds."

Any final comments?

TM: "There is one idea I have that I believe the music industry really must implement. We need to instigate a mandatory retirement age for rockers, maybe somewhere around thirty-five or thirty-six. Some people will slip through the cracks, like Neil Young, who are still making some kind of vital music, and it would be a shame to lose them, but it would be for the greater good of getting rid of all the horrible old time rockers who keep coming back with these reunion tours.

"The reason I make the suggestion is because of an Aerosmith article I recently read in *Pulse* magazine. I once loved Aerosmith, but there are times when rock musicians become an embarrassment to their craft. In the interview, Steven Tyler referred to their song 'Let the Music Do the Talking' from a few records ago, and said, 'That is the kind of music I love and represents what Aerosmith really is.' The interviewer then asks, 'Why don't you play that kind of music?' Steve responded, 'We put the song out and even had a video, but it did not sell. Therefore we brought in all these song doctors and people who write the perfect pop radio hit to help us make some pop gems to sell the albums so we can do the music that we really like on the other songs.' What kind of (expletive) is that? They are supposed to be the seminal hard rock band, but if those are the seminal hard rock values, then the form is utterly void of merit. It makes it that much more blatantly obvious that music is just a product to be sold like a brand of cereal. I am done venting. Thank you."

[Originally printed in September/October '93 Issue #43]

"The Bible is one of the world's most read pieces of literature. Whether I believe in it or not is an entirely different question altogether."

—Kirk Hammett

{ METALLICA }

2

Here's a glimpse at thrash metal's most popular band: Metallica. Phil Chalmers (of True Lies video series fame) caught up with guitarist Kirk Hammett in 1991 and recorded the conversation. Listen in:

Okay, I'm going to ask you about some of your songs ... Let's start with the song "Jump In The Fire."

KM: "I can't remember how the lyrics go, but they're probably what you think they are about."

It seems like it's talking about Satan. It says: *Jump by your will, or you will be taken by force/ I'll get you either way.*

KM: "Yeah, that was real immature. I mean, we will never do anything like that ever again."

"Seek And Destroy"...

KM: "That's just about having a lot of fun. You're not supposed to take it literally."

How about "Fade to Black?"

KM: "That's about a person who is really depressed, and he's trapped in this depressed state. A lot of people think it promotes suicide. I don't think it does."

At the end it says, *Nobody but me can save myself/ But it's too late/ Death greets me warm/ Now I will just say goodbye* ... How do you deal with people who say this song is causing kids to take their life?

KM: "We can't be responsible for everyone's mental state of mind. If people single out that song as a reason for them to take their life, or using it to justify their decision to take their life—that's wrong."

I want to run a case by you that happened in my area here. A kid took his life and had your lyrics in his suicide letter. He said that basically he was suicidal, and this song kinda summed up what he wanted to do. I guess it kinda pushed him over the edge. How do you respond to that?

KM: "It's a horrible thing to be in this position, but, you know, you can't be responsible for everyone. We are in no way in control of other people's psychosis. A person is a master of their own destiny. There's no way that we could stop it. If we did have control over it, we'd obviously say, 'This is just a song. It's not meant to be taken literally.' If a kid is very suicidal and he doesn't get the proper help and takes his life, whose fault is it? Is it the kid's fault, the parent's fault, or our fault?"

What is your main goal as a rock band?

KM: "To play good music and to make a statement of some sort. I know a lot of the stuff we say is dark, and it isn't very positive, but the usual, normal, healthy person can differentiate from that. We are not telling people to do anything at all. We're not preaching. We're not using our popularity as a platform."

Do you feel you have an accountability to your audience?

KM: "Yeah, but only to an extent."

How do you feel about all the negativism in rock 'n' roll, like the satanic, the violence, and the pro-suicide messages?

KM: "I'm the type of person that could take it or leave it. Like Satanism: There's two sides of it. You have your satanic bands, like Slayer and Venom, and then you have your anti-satanic bands, like Stryper and whoever else. Who is doing good and who is doing bad is in the eye of the beholder. Is any band right for doing what they do? If they want to shove their ethics down people's throats, that's fine with me, but as a person who's in control of my own choices, I'm just not going to pay attention to either of it, because I don't think either of it is worth more merit than the other."

What is your philosophy of life?

KM: "I'm pro-human. I'm pro-humanitarian. I'm pretty aware of what goes on around me."

What religious background do you come from?

KM: "Catholicism."

Are you a practicing Catholic right now?

KM: "Not a practicing ... If you want my religious idea, I believe there is a supreme being ... a supreme energy; it's like a big mesh of religions."

How do you feel about Jesus Christ?

KM: "I don't know if He actually was ever here. I just know I believe in a supreme being."

Are you happy with your life right now, Kirk?

KM: "Yeah."

What do you base your happiness on?

KM: "I have goals to look forward to, and I'm accomplishing a lot of goals. I'm at a point where I could have a lot, but I don't ask for a lot."

If you die today, what happens?

KM: "I'd make sure I'd get cremated."

After you get cremated, then what?

KM: "So, in other words, you're asking me if I believe in life after death? You know, it's the eternal mystery. No one knows any more than anyone else does."

Have you ever read the Bible?

KM: "Yeah, I went to a Catholic school."

Do you believe the Bible?

KM: "The Bible is one of the world's most read pieces of literature. Whether I believe in it or not is an entirely different question altogether. I tend to view it as more of a literary piece than anything else."

What would you say to someone who said Jesus Christ died on a cross for your sins, and you had to make a decision to accept Christ, and if you didn't, you'd be burning in the lake of fire for eternity?

KM: "That's an unfair assumption."

Why?

KM: "Because I don't think that anyone living would have any sort of decision like that over anyone dead."

Would you like to say anything to our readers, which are predominantly Christians?

KM: "It's interesting talking to people who are so devout. I'm not as devout, obviously, as your readers. I'm a person with my own views and my own outlooks, and I feel strongly about my opinions. And, I feel strongly about the band's approach to certain things."

[Originally printed in December/January '91 Issue #27]

"If someone finds comfort in praying to God every night, that's his business, and I would never criticize him for it."

—Greg Graffin

BAD RELIGION

3

When the punk rock movement exploded in the late '70s and early '80s, numerous groups like the Sex Pistols, Black Flag, and the Dead Kennedys so influenced the scene that they earned legendary status. However, while all of the above groups are no longer together, one legendary punk band called Bad Religion has kept going, making them the only true living legend punk band. Vocalist Greg Graffin, who was only fifteen when Bad Religion began, spoke with HM writer David Jenison in 1993 about the ideas and message of Bad Religion's music.

I really like your new album, but it sounds somewhat different than your previous albums. How have your fans been responding to the new material?

GG: "We just got back from a six-week European tour, and our fans there gave us an incredible response. Everyone loved the new material. Our U.S. tour is about to begin, and I expect that our fans in America will love the new material just as much."

I hear that you are a professor at Cornell University. Is this true?

GG: "Almost. I am working on a Ph.D. in evolutionary biology at Cornell, but I am not quite a professor yet. I do teach classes in comparative biology, though."

How far away are you from your degree?

GG: "If I wasn't in Bad Religion, I would be finished within a year. However, it won't happen this year because Bad Religion is seriously interfering with my research."

Which is more of a priority, Bad Religion or Cornell?

GG: "Right now Bad Religion is a career for me, while academia is a career I can enter when I am older. I hope that I'll still be able to do Bad Religion when I am older, but you never know, do you?"

Being a student of evolution, what is your opinion of the Creationist movement?

GG: "Part of the reason I started studying evolution comes from the ideas of Creationism. I am not very religious, obviously, but I think that everybody is curious about where they came from. I asked some of the basic questions about our origin, and God could not answer them for me, so I consulted textbooks and looked to fossils for the answers."

What do you feel about the Creationist teachers like those at the Creation Research Institute?

GG: "Anytime a person tells someone how to think and that his way is best while everyone else is wrong, he pretty much falls into the category of 'bad religion.' We have always written against such people, because they infringe on the free thinking of others. To me, it is not really an issue of who's right and who's wrong, but how we can deal with our origin. It is such a nebulas concept that a person almost has to have his own personal understanding of it. Origin is something a person must come to terms with as a person and not as a group.

"Creationists cannot be argued with, because they say that there is a God and He made us. I am suggesting that, if there is a God, why doesn't He make Himself apparent? How can we believe this God created us when we cannot even put our finger on Him? However, we can put our finger on aspects of evolution, and we can study the distribution of species, recognizing that certain species are more closely related than others. We can come up with a coherent theory that is testable about how we came to be. Though scientific study makes much more sense, the idea of origin is still a personal phenomenon. It is how you deal with it yourself."

I know you recently played at a pro-choice benefit concert with White Zombie and Stone Temple Pilots. Since you are a biologist, I would appreciate your commentary on the abortion issue.

GG: "I am very strongly pro-choice, though not because it is a male-female issue, but because it is a human issue. People should be given the right to do what they want with their bodies, and there shouldn't be anyone interfering with that freedom. In fact, I think it is ludicrous and upsetting that people would even try to interfere. Furthermore, I would feel horrible if something should happen to my wife, and she would not be allowed to have an abortion. This comes from someone who has a child and another one on the way.

"Concerning the idea that abortion is an issue of murder, I disagree. Murder is a concept that was devised to allow people to fit into society, which makes murder a social issue. Embryos are not a part of our society, so they cannot be grouped within the social ethics of murder. Embryos are completely dependent and developing creatures. Therefore, since the fetus is absolutely dependent upon the mother, the rights of the mother are all that should be concerned.

"A question that does arise, however, is where the line should be drawn. Well, there are viable fetuses being born at the six and seven month mark. Therefore, I would hope that anyone considering an abortion would do it well in advance of that time, because by then all the higher neuro-functions are in place and the fetus can begin to feel. We do want to be humane about it, don't we?"

Many of your songs, like "American Jesus," discuss the relationship between government and religion. Would you mind commenting on this connection?

GG: "Our song 'American Jesus' talks about how absurd it is to think that our God is better than someone else's. It is also absurd to think that Jesus is totally inseparable from the American way of life. From a very young age, people are told that America allows you to think freely and that there is religious freedom. These are great constitutional tenets of America, but they are seldom seen in practice. How many Muslim presidents do you think we will have? Probably not very many. The unspoken truth is that the American dream is built on Christianity.

"Many people think that Jesus is responsible for all the good in America. If so, then Jesus has to be responsible for all the bad in America too. I wonder, though, why a God that is all kind and all good would allow the things to happen which are happening in America."

Are your criticisms against the Church's actions, against its theology, or both?

GG: "I would not go so far as to say that I am against theology. Remember, though, you would get a different opinion from different members of the band. I write a little over half the songs, Brett writes a little under half, and the other guys write a small percentage of the rest. You would get a different opinion depending on which songwriter you are talking to and to which song you are referring.

"In my opinion, the one evil in America is the same evil that a person will find in any country—and that is simple ignorance. People who only think one way, who try to get others to think like they do, and who are insistent that their way is best are really the most ignorant people in the world. Their actions show that they have not had the time or the desire to see things from both sides.

"Our ability to rationalize and to use our conscious mind is an essential quality of being human. Indeed, it is such a basic trait of the human mind that I am amazed how often it goes wasted. People are often like animals in that they have the horde mentality, always thinking as a group. The one characteristic that sets humans apart from animals is our ability to be individuals, and that not only means thinking uniquely, but allowing others to be individuals and to think uniquely as well."

What do you think about a Christian who is open-minded and does not push his beliefs on other people?

GG: "I think that's fine. In fact, theology is like that. I have known theologians, and I respect them because they are scholars. They are people who are inquisitive and that are seeking knowledge. If someone finds comfort in praying to God every night, that's his business, and I would never criticize him for it."

In other words, you are only criticizing the people who shove it on others?

GG: "Exactly. I think that is ignorance coming out. It is people looking for a cause. It is not just Christianity that does this, though. It is all the circles of religion with all their written and unwritten laws to which a person must subscribe. Jews are the same way. I am not Jewish, but Brett and Greg are, and they really hate their upbringing."

Were Greg and Brett raised strict Jews?

GG: "No, but they were definitely raised in the Jewish community. I know Brett went to Synagogue and even had a Bar Mitzvah."

Basically, would you say that you are an atheist?

GG: "Atheist is too strong a title. I assume when you say 'atheist,' you mean a person that knows there is no God. According to that description, atheism is a religion unto itself. Because of my hesitation to label myself to a member of a religion, I hesitate to take that title.

"I am very inquisitive and very curious, but I have never found a question answered better by God than answered by science. I guess, in that respect, science has become a religion to me, but only because it is based on testable hypothesis. Religion, on the other hand, is based on faith, saying, 'If you believe, then it's true."

Are you open to the possibility of a divinity?

GG: "I don't know if divinity is the right word. In terms of powers greater than myself, definitely, but that power or force is not preordained by any one being with a white beard. In other words, I don't believe that power is a god."

Within a belief structure that has no type of god or superpower, what determines the standard for ethical decisions?

GG: "What is the basis for ethical decisions? Unfortunately, it is determined by the government, and if the government is based on religion, as ours is based on Christianity, then the religion seems to determine the ethics. Furthermore, ethics are historical entities, meaning they are based on some standard that is determined by the founding fathers. It seems that the history of a country, or the history of the lifestyle in that country, influences what people believe is ethically correct. It is like whatever our founding fathers decided to do, the way our ancestors decided to live their lives, reflects how we should determine our ethics.

"There is an extreme difference in ethics from one country to the next. For example, I am sure that we would not understand many things that go on in India or in the small countries in Africa. The extremity of the differences implies that ethics are actually random. We are all living and breathing humans with the same physiology, but our ethics are so different. Therefore, I believe that ethics should not be based on religion. Rather, whatever is controlling our biology, that which makes us the same, is what should control our ethics. It is possible to live without religion in a country yet still retain a keen sense of its history."

I am curious about whether you were raised in a religious home.

GG: "No, my parents never took me to be baptized. My mother was from a really strict religious family, so I think that is why she raised me away from church."

Any final comments?

GG: "People should know that we do not hate them for being religious. We do not rail on people because they are Christians, but because they are closed-minded. Regretfully, within Christianity, the close-minded belief structure is built-in. It disturbs me, because it seems like a person can only live the American dream if he's rich and Christian. I guess that makes him the ultimate American, doesn't it?"

[Originally printed in November/December '93 Issue #44]

"I don't have
a problem
with Jesus.
'Jesus is just
alright with me,'
you know,
The Doobie
Brothers."

—Bruce Kulick

KISS {4}

photo by Lisa Johnson

In 1994, after being around twenty years, Kiss was still huge, kickin' like a
hungry young band with something to say. It's no small feat to keep a band
going that long, especially when it's taken a band through its makeup
phase, the disco era, and then having to earn respect on music without the
aid of makeup. Kiss has influenced millions of listeners and hundreds of
musicians—including Garth Brooks, Extreme, Faith No More, Rage Against
The Machine, and Anthrax, all of whom were recording Kiss covers for a
Kiss tribute album at the time of this interview. Because of this huge influence on both the music scene and the teenage population, it was high time
for HM to get on the phone with 'em for an interview. Guitarist Bruce Kulick
answers questions about being role models and the Christian rock scene.

Is the new album going to sound similar to the *Revenge* album?

BK: "That's a good question. I would definitely say it's going to have a lot of the attitude. I hate to use the word 'heavy,' but I will say it's guitar and riff driven. It's kind of still early to talk about it, because we have been spending a lot of time on material. Gene has quite a few heavy songs, kind of dark, heavy, moody stuff. It's definitely going to be along the lines of *Revenge* in the sense that there's going to be a lot of riffs. It's certainly not going to be a pop record."

What do you think of the tag that Kiss has received over the years as being an evil band, like the "Knights In Satan's Service" acronym?

BK: "We don't seem to get it as much. I know when I first joined, I was shocked. There's no doubt that Gene in makeup and his whole image and what he was putting out onstage was certainly ... to me it was more of a character from a comic book or something—'The Demon,' and 'Paul, the Star Child.' It was all incredible fantasy. Let's face it, it was like fantasy come to life for impressing kids. These guys were not in any way evil, and I knew that. It's just your stick to express yourself. It's your other side. It's kind of like Dr. Jekyll and Mr. Hyde.

"When I was on tour with them, there was no makeup anymore, which really didn't make Gene very 'evil' anymore, if you know what I mean. To see these people come out like that ... I didn't understand it. Very religious people sometimes are frightened by things that they don't understand, or they think it really is legitimately that way, or they think that he's going back to his hotel room and sacrificing lambs in his room or lighting candles, when all we're doing is watching CNN and ordering room service. And hey, if he wants to have a girl in his room, that's his business—he's not married. I never could understand it, but I guess it comes with the territory.

"I do feel that everyone should have the right to express, you know, what they want and what they're doing. Certainly nowadays there's things like *Beavis and Butthead* and people like that, which people are in uproar about, that I think are even more intense than anything Kiss ever got into."

How do you respond to someone who says, "You need to be careful to be a good example for kids, because they sure look up to ya?"

BK: "I understand that. I have relatives that are of the age that I would hate for them to take something from either *Beavis and Butthead* or something Kiss says too literally or seriously. I think kids are not stupid. I really think that they can decide where the edge is and where not to fall off—if they're smart. It doesn't take a lot for them to be smart.

"Your friends saying, 'Yeah, let's do something stupid!' I think peer pressure and things like that—those are more evil than bands or *Beavis and Butthead*. There's always those elements that are going to draw you into bad kids that don't know anything but to be bad. I don't think it has anything to do with groups. Some of the rap music is a little extreme, I've got to admit.

"Take Body Count's song 'Cop Killer,' for example. I would hope they're understanding that it's artistic freedom and talking about that they're frustrated about cops being bad to black people, so that's why they want to sing about killing a cop. I don't think that's really right, but I would hope a black kid doesn't take that seriously and want to kill a cop. Just like if we're talking about love being great and babes being cool, that you don't—in the day of AIDS—go out and sleep with every girl you meet and be promiscuous. We're not trying to tell anybody to do anything.

"You turn on television and it's everywhere. Sometimes the more you keep it in the closet or try to lock it up under lock and key, the more they want it. Obviously, if they choose it, I think it has more to do with something lacking in them as a person. They need to understand that they need to grow. (It's) not the fact that they're exposed to it. It's everywhere. If you're a parent, you never curse in front of your kids. What, do you think they don't hear curse words in school? They do. The kids love to talk about it, because they know it's something that's bad. I'm aware (that) you guys ... it's like a Christian rock magazine, right?"

Yeah.

BK: "I'm sure you probably deal with a lot of these issues. I still really feel that the most important thing is that love (from) parents and giving them the kind of understanding that keeps a kid from choosing what's right and what's wrong and making their choices in life. I think we're living in a very difficult time. I think things are more complicated than they were twenty years ago."

How do you feel about someone mixing very heavy music with very happy lyrics or attitude?

BK: "In some ways, it doesn't really work. I don't know why. To be honest with you, I wasn't a fan of Stryper, moreso because it was just too—forgetting the lyrics, because I don't always listen to lyrics—it was just too pop for me to begin with, even though they were playing crunchy guitars and everything.

"I look at The Beatles as a great example. You can't have a better song writing repertoire than a group like The Beatles. Like, when they did *Helter Skelter*, the music represented kind of like what they were singing about. You don't wanna sing 'Black Bird' over those kind of chord changes, with the guitars distorted and all. In good song writing—this has nothing to do with religious songs or not in good song writing—I always feel that the chords and the attitude of how you present that does have an influence on what you should be singing about. They have to kind of fit."

You kind of touched on my next question. I was going to ask you what you think of the Christian rock music you've heard.

BK: "I tell you, the only band I'm really aware of is Stryper. You know who I am a big fan of, that I'm aware are born again Christians, is King's X. I think they're excellent. I know the whole band feels this way—Gene is a big fan, and so is Paul and Eric. We're very disappointed that they weren't really able to break. I'm not sure why. I know it doesn't have anything to do with (being) Christian or anything like that, but they're excellent. They're really excellent. Great guitarist, good song writing. I hate to say it, but could it be that it's because they didn't come out with aggressive enough music, maybe? You don't know. I don't think they're over. I think if they keep doing it, something will happen.

"I think that right now kids are responding to ... like I referred to before, it's a very difficult time right now, the way the world is. Things are pretty out of hand in some ways, between the riots in L.A. and the economy. You still have war over in Europe. Certain things have gotten better, but certainly domestically people are tighter financially, and I think the whole race issue is way more extreme now than it ever was, maybe. I think that's why bands like Nirvana and Pearl Jam—moody, kind of like darker, tougher bands— have exploded. You notice that a lot of the fluffy kind of pop rock groups are history.

"It does go in cycles. You'll see, there'll be a huge band in the 1990s that is going to sound like Journey probably, and I like that kind of music too. I do like Nirvana and Pearl Jam and that stuff, but you look at where the bands are at that are selling lots of records right now, and you realize in some ways the kids don't want 'Mr. Cool Groovy Rock Star' that's got poofy hair and is singing about love and roses. The only bands that are singing about love and stuff like that are kind of like quirky hippie looking, and that's rebellious.

"It just seems like a lot of the bands that really make it big are on the edge. I don't think you have to be, but lately they seem to be one step in the grave kind of thing. That's why I always think that Christian rock is kind of like two opposite things; although I don't think that you have to be a heroin addict to be a talented musician and be in a famous rock band, but it sometimes kind of goes with the territory. I think Kiss is an excellent role model in the sense of, at least the current Kiss, being four guys who just love playing music and are very straight. You're not going to find one of us in the gutter, because we just love our lives the way we are, and we don't need those crutches.

"People judge me. They say, 'Oh, he's the guitarist for Kiss. He must cheat on his wife. He must be a drug addict. He's probably so loaded that he doesn't give a [expletive] about anything. He has wild, drunken parties.' None of that's true, you see. A lot of these perceptions about rock and roll—I can't say they aren't true (laughs). They're just not true for me.

"I'm not sure what's big in the Christian rock scene. Maybe there are some other groups, I don't know. I've always found that it's hard for me to get a grasp of that, although I don't have a problem with that. How do they deal with that? Playing music now that sounds so grungy too ... So, how do you sing about your devotion to Christ or whatever it is that you are religiously speaking of, and the music's going, 'Dan-gung-gung-gung-gung' with all these D-tuned low chords? I mean, they really sound more like Godzilla walking down the block.

"I never look at any of the dark stuff being devil stuff, but of course there are bands that like to call themselves 'Death' and 'Cancer' and those kind of words. I guess it's all to express themselves. It's all a matter of expression— all this music. It really doesn't matter, as long as you're expressing yourself. I like to take in a lot of different music. There's something I always like in all of them. The bands I really can't deal with are some of those death metal bands. I don't get anything musically out of it. I think the kids that are into that ... the only way they can communicate is they have their heads pounded. That's what they get from the music—their heads are being pounded. I don't know. Are there any Christian rock bands that sound like Death?"

Yeah. There are.

BK: "Are they just pounding them with Jesus, though?"

Or talking about how Jesus was murdered and killed.

BK: "That's interesting. None of those thrash bands have really broken anyway—Christian or not. Still, all the bands that really are new and sound extreme still have songs. It's still a song. Stone Temple Pilots—I think they're tremendous. Why? Because there are three or four songs on that first album that are really great—really catchy, melodic, I can relate to it. The same thing with Pearl Jam's first record. Nirvana—even though there's some tracks in there that give me a headache, there's great stuff on that record. That's the other key—there's attitude, but you've gotta have a great song that everyone kind of falls into, and it moves them. Maybe that's what King's X needs to do. I don't think they need to worry about talent. They've got it. It's that song that gets everybody.

"Alright. You got enough there?"

Well, actually I've got a couple more questions.

BK: "Alright, let's do it quick."

How do you feel about Jesus Christ?

BK: "How do I feel about ... That's a good question. It's an interesting question. I mean, I'm Jewish actually. Although I married a Christian. She's not Catholic, but she's Christian. In fact, I was married in a Christian church. I had a rabbi present, though, too. I don't view Jesus Christ as God. I view God, the One above Jesus Christ, as my God. But I don't have any disrespect for Jesus Christ.

"As a kid, there were Catholic school kids that used to try to beat up and chase me. 'Let's kill the Jew! He killed our God! He killed Jesus!' Which really makes you screwed up when you're growing up, because you're going, 'Huh? What did I do? Wait a minute! Jesus was a Jew! I don't get it!' Not to really get into a whole religious thing ...

"I say, 'He is the Son of God,' but I view God ... I view them as kind of the same, although you may not; or someone who is very into Jesus doesn't. But, where my kind of inter-religious beliefs come from is really not the New Testament. It's really the Old Testament, but it's really all the same thing. It's still the Judeo-Christian ethics, I have them. I try to follow them the best I can. I don't like to lie and cheat and commit adultery and murder and all those things. I think that's all that really matters.

"Whether or not it's Jesus Christ or God or you want to pray to Moses or Buddha or whoever it is, I think as long as your senses realize that there is something greater out there and, regardless if you want to call it 'fear of Him'—just respect of all that—then do it. If you don't believe in any religion, I don't care. I don't have a problem with it. What I do have problems with is people who shake fingers at other people, and abortion, you know, and get crazy with all that. That stuff I don't like. I don't have a problem with Jesus. 'Jesus is just alright with me,' you know, The Doobie Brothers. (laughs)

"I tell ya, Gene's the one you want to get into an interview with if you want to get into religious stuff, because he went to religious school when he was young. He'd chew your ear off with the [expletive]. It's too much. He gets into it, like ridiculous."

That'd be fun to sit down with him sometime and get into it.

BK: "I wouldn't want to be there."

How do your beliefs on this affect your daily life?

BK: "Well, I just feel that I was brought up with the right ethics from my parents. Whether that's because I'm Jewish or it was from that whole Judeo-Christian thing, I don't think about it often. I know that sometimes, when I'm upset enough, I realize I've gotta relax. Sometimes you want to close your eyes and think about a higher state that you're feeling that there's somebody there that won't make everything terrible for you. You've gotta have that feeling sometimes. I don't consider myself a very religious person, you see what I mean?

"In some ways I do want to think that everything happens for a reason, and maybe when something bad happens that it's God's will. So, I only think of it in those terms—to cool me out. You hate going through life blaming people and events. You have to realize that maybe you're responsible. It helps me get through life. Like I said, I don't think I'm very religious, I'm just aware of those ethics that I grew up with."

What do you think about the claims of Christ, where He said, "I am the only way to the Father, and no one comes to Him but by Me"?

BK: "Umm. You're saying that, if I don't call Jesus Christ my Savior, then whenever that's supposed to happen, that I won't go?"

Well, basically, I'm asking about the claims He made about Himself when He was talking to Jews, that "I am the Way to the Father. No one comes to Him but by Me."

BK: "See, I wasn't taught that kind of stuff. I went to Hebrew school, and I was Bar Mitzvah-ed and everything. If you're growing up being taught nothing really about Jesus Christ, then none of that really makes sense to you. That stuff doesn't make sense to me and I don't ... Again, I respect born again Christians and Christianity, but I don't buy that it's the way to believe. Just like I wouldn't tell a Buddhist, 'Hey, why don't you pray to God? Become a Jew and convert this way.' I think everyone should have their own thing, so that doesn't work for me. It's not like I hate you for it or I have a problem with it. I don't care. Just don't try to sell it to me. Jews don't go around trying to get other people to convert. The only time they want to convert someone is for marriage, when they realize, 'I want to be with them!' If you want to look at it strict: Even if a woman does convert to Judaism, the child really isn't Jewish. You've got to be born Jewish or whatever.

"You're telling me that ... I didn't know about that, to be honest with you. I'm not a real expert to talk about it."

When I became a Christian, I almost overnight had an immediate great respect and love for the Jewish people, because I see them as my people now, and I'm part of the same big family. I'd love to apologize to you for those Catholic boys who tried to beat you up, 'cause that's ...

BK: "Well, thanks. I know what you're saying. That's all ignorance. I realize it too. I didn't understand it when I was young, but hey, while they were out busy being bullies, I was getting an education. I was sitting home playing guitar. I was doing good in school. Even if I didn't want to do good in school, I was fortunate that I had a God-given gift of music that somehow the guitar could kind of flow through me. I was doing that. I was sitting at home transfixed with this music and plugging into that. The kids that were running around beating up Jews, they're just bullies. They don't get it. They don't realize that they don't even understand the issue. I don't think even the person that was teaching them was teaching them *that* kind of thing.

[Originally printed in January/February '94 Issue #45]

"I try to take
any great man
that's ever
walked this planet,
that has had
something good
to say, then
I read about him,
it affects me,
and I'm in."

—Sammy Hagar

Following is the uncut/unedited/but sometimes censored interview we did with Sammy Hagar—the man who went from solo artist to Van Halen frontman back to solo artist.

Let me say that I love this new album. I think you did a great job. I remember on the *Standing Hampton* tour, you used to come out for your encore and say, "We're gonna do a song by the greatest rock 'n' roll band ever," and you'd launch into "Whole Lotta Love." And I think you captured the spirit of that band with "Little White Lie."

SH: "I wouldn't see that connection, but you know, like, when you just do something, like in a second, it came so fast, I just did it, I didn't think about it, you know ... I would imagine. You're probably right, if I took every element even. Probably on the next tour, when I go out, I'll say, 'Yeah, I'll do a song by the greatest rock 'n' roll band who ever lived,' and I'll bust into 'Dreams' by Van Halen."

So, did you enjoy getting back into the solo thing in the studio, and having full control?

SH: "Yeah, I really did. Being in a band for eleven years, it was great, first of all. You know, no complaints, no nothing. It just was a great movie with a bad ending. Everything was great until the end. Unfortunately, sometimes that happens. But with Van Halen, there was always a compromise. I'd say, 'I wanna paint that wall blue,' and Eddie would go, 'I don't know, maybe red,' and Alex would go, 'Naw, black,' you know, and Mike would go, 'I don't know, white,' and you end up with a brown wall. And that's what bands are about. That's what Zeppelin was about, that's what The Who was about. All those bands are like that. Otherwise, if there's a leader that gets his way all the time, then it's a solo artist. Then you've got John Fogerty. He's the same with Credence as he was solo. It's just no difference. So being a solo artist, you don't ever have to ask anybody. You've just gotta say, 'This is what I want to do.' And there's a great, great freedom to that, and I'd forgotten how fast you can get things done, how fast you can move. For Van Halen, we used to take two months to decide what producer we were gonna use, three or four months sometimes. We couldn't even get started on a record. As a solo artist, you just say, 'Hey, I wanna use this guy. He's available? Okay, when can he start? Tomorrow? Okay.' Everything happened so much quicker, and it makes everything real fresh and exciting. I'm lovin' it right now, I mean, the freedom is killing me, man. I'm just going, 'Oh boy, this is a blast!' and probably five years from now, I'll be going, 'Where's my band members, man?'"

I think the excitement is kind of contagious. It kind of came across on these songs.

SH: "These songs are the freshest thing I've ever done in my whole career. I'm just telling you straight up, and they are fresh! I wrote the songs and recorded 'em, and they were done. Nothing was pre-written, except 'Amnesty is Granted,' which is an old song I wrote a couple years ago. And the other song was 'Warmth of the Womb,' I had written about two months before the band split. I wrote it for Van Halen. But everything else, man, I just wrote as I was recording. I just went along ... and then they're on MTV talking about me. And some guy yells at me, 'Sammy, Sammy, hey, you gotta see the brothers on TV!' And so I come running out of the studio into the lounge, and there they are, man. And I'm going, 'What? These guys are lying. That's not what happened. Aww, come on!' So I wrote 'Little White Lie.' That's how fresh this record was. Everything that happened, I wrote about. My wife had a baby, I wrote a song. It was pretty special doing it that way."

My favorite Sammy Hagar album, what was it called, *All Night Long*? That live album that came out years ago.

SH: "That had some energy man. I listened to that record just last year, and I couldn't believe it. I'm going, 'This guy's jacked out of his brain!' A lot of energy on that record. That's a real live record, too, you know; there's no fixing up, no overdubs, no nothing."

That's a true live record, as it ran. I like this one even better than that.

SH: "Well, thank you very much. This album is pure Sammy Hagar. This should have the scratch and sniff on it—it smells like me, man! Right now, it's my favorite record I've ever made in my whole life, and that's a big statement, because *5150* and For *Unlawful Carnal Knowledge*, those were great, great, great records. I would've never thought I could've outdone those, but in my heart, I did on this record."

What was it like playing with the guys in Montrose again, and some of the other players you worked with on this album?

SH: "It was great. You know, Ronnie Montrose played really, really good on that song. I'm really impressed with that. Denny Carmassi is one of the great rock drummers of all time. That's that Led Zeppelin thing in this album, that's probably what you hear is that Denny, man, playing that big (expletive) bass sound. He's got a great foot on him. And Bootsy Collins, what an experience. On 'Would You Do It For Free?' I wrote that song on bass, and Bootsy ... there was a toss up in my head of who I would ask to play on it, whether it would be Flea or Bootsy, because they're the two baddest bass players I know. And a friend of mine says, 'Man, you should get the grand daddy of funk. Get Bootsy to play.' And I go, 'Do you know Bootsy?' He goes, 'Yeah,' and I said, '(expletive).' So he grabbed the telephone and called him up. That was a great experience, hearing a guy that was that much of a master on his instrument. It's like Eddie on guitar, you know; Eddie's a master of that guitar, and Bootsy's a master of the bass. We cut that song— Denny Carmassi, Bootsy on bass, and me on guitar—and it was just rippin', man. I mean, it was almost like we didn't even have to do any of the overdubs. We had the song just like that. Oh, and Mickey Hart, my newfound best friend in the world, my mentor, my hero, man, I love this guy. He's got more energy and enthusiasm than any human being I've ever met in my life. If I play him a riff—I could just be sitting around on the guitar and play one lick—and he'll go, 'Hey! Do that again! If you play that and I play the beat like this to it, see whatcha got?' And I'd go, 'Whoa! No (expletive)!' I never would've thought of it like that. That's just a blues lick.' Like 'Marching to Mars,' I'm just playing a 'School's Out' blues, you know, Alice Cooper sound type lick. That's just an old blues lick, and this guy heard this kind of a beat behind it, and next thing you know, you've got this almost high tech drum beat behind this blues lick. I just can't believe it, the guy's just so energetic and enthusiastic, that he just pulls something outta nothing. There's a song called 'Ether,' and it's only on the Japanese version, I think. It's just a little one-minute instrumental, I think. But I wrote that about Mickey, how out of thin air, this guy can just pull something out. He's really amazing."

How has being a father changed your outlook?

SH: "Well, I've been a father, but being a new father of a baby girl—my first baby girl, I've got two sons—I'm tellin' ya, the best way I could sum it up is that moment when your baby is born ... everyone in life is looking for a miracle. You know, you want to see somebody fly? You want to see someone walk on water? You want to think someone can just do something that no one else can—to perform a miracle. But when you see that baby come out, and you realize it was inside of its mother for all that time, it grew, you know, and now you cut the cord and it takes its first breath, that's like a whole different dimension. And when you see that, you realize that is truly a miracle. And that blows your mind so bad that you kind of become enlightened. It changes your life. I think it does; it did me again. It just enlightened me to the fact that life is a miracle. The fact that I'm sitting here talking to you on the telephone is a miracle. It makes you a little more enlightened to where everything you see around you, you take a little more seriously, and all of a sudden you feel like you're responsible for this baby, and you're so in love with this baby, the fact that you would take a bullet for this baby, and not even complain. You know, 'Save this baby's life? Take mine right now!' And when you start thinking like that, you realize that's the true meaning of love, and that's what love is. It's unconditional. You don't take love from someone. That's what love is all about. I mean, when you give love, more flows through you, and it becomes a special, special thing. And when you start living your life like that, about giving and not taking, and about caring, and being unselfish and not even thinking of yourself, you'd be amazed how beautiful life is. And that's how it changed my life."

I can definitely concur with that. About a year ago, we had our first child. It was a baby girl, we had the birth at home, and I caught the baby ...

SH: "Oh, come on, then you know exactly what I'm talking about! You know, you love that baby. When's her birthday?"

February 25.

SH: "Oh yeah, Kama's is April 1. So the song, when I wrote the song 'Kama,' you know, that's my baby's name, and it means 'love' in Sanskrit, the original written language. And that's supposed to be the true way to say the word 'love,' like you, know, 'love' is the American version, or 'amore,' and all these things, but you know, Kama is the true meaning, as in Kama Sutra, which is 'the art of love,' and the art of lovemaking. (laughs) I think it's been turned into that, but I think Kama Sutra actually means the 'art of love.' So Kama comes from that. And that song, when I wrote that song, I just closed my eyes, and I just wrote about exactly what happened. You should listen to that song and think about the birth of your baby, and about naming it, and about what you're feeling. That song will take your (expletive) South. If you don't get choked up when you know what that song's about, then you'll have to convince me that you had a baby."

We named our daughter Kaela.

SH: "Wow, that's totally similar. Does it mean something?"

No, we just took a name from the Bible, and kind of adapted it to the spelling we wanted.

SH: "I bet it means something. Kaela, I bet, whatever the original spelling was, if it came from the Bible, it means something. Check it out. A name has power. Words have power. They work. That's why poetry can affect people. That's why music and lyrics and songs affect people, and that's why chants and prayers and affirmations, and all these various things affect the frame of mind. And a name, this person goes through their whole life and people call them that name. And a name like (expletive), the poor kid would be pretty torn up, you know, 'I don't feel very good about myself, you know, everybody yells (expletive) at me.' I think it's cool to have a good name."

I agree wholeheartedly. What's funny, you know, here's this redheaded rocker, and he's no longer working with this big band, Van Halen, and he's singing a song about forgiveness in "Amnesty is Granted." What's up with that?

SH: "Well, I actually wrote that song while I was in Van Halen. This is a long story, but the reason it's on this album is because this album is truly a concept record about what happened. 'Marching to Mars' is the concept about, 'Hey, I'm leaving it behind. I'm moving on. I know there's life in the universe for Sammy Hagar, and I'm gonna live it.'

"'Amnesty is Granted' wasn't written for the bereavement. It's on this record because it is a statement to these guys. I still love Ed now. I don't love the managers; I wish I could. (laughs) If I was really Christ-like, I could, but I can't muster it up to love their manager. But I still love Ed now, and when I think of Van Halen, I think of some great times. I think that Eddie and I wrote some of the greatest songs ever written in rock 'n' roll in the last ten years, and I really feel like amnesty is granted. I don't like what they did. I think it was a chicken (expletive) move, but at the same time, I still love them. I would rather run into them in the street somewhere and give 'em a big hug, and go out and have a beer, and talk about good times, rather than just get in a fist fight. That's the way I would like to think of Van Halen. That's why 'Amnesty is Granted' is on this album in that specific place, right before 'Marching to Mars.'"

A lot of the songs on here kind of reflect a Judeo-Christian outlook. Have there been any changes in Sammy Hagar's life since ...

SH: "Not really. I've always been a real positive person. I like to bring hope and happiness to people, and maybe some direction to people, rather than doom and gloom. I just think the world is as ugly as we see it. The only 'Christian' part of me is what we talked about before, with the love, which is ... I'm not an organized religious guy at all. I don't go to church at all. I believe in prayer. I believe in the power of it, that it has power if you pray and project positive thoughts, there is power there, and that's a good thing. The love side, about unconditional love, which is the Christ philosophy, that you give love, unselfish love—forgiveness, amnesty, that kind of thing—but I have Buddhist philosophies, and I have Zen philosophies, and I have Krishna philosophies. That's just me. That's what I'm made up of. And what I try to do, is I try to take any great man that's ever walked this planet, that has had something good to say, then I read about him, it affects me, and I'm in. I'm going, 'Hey, I'll take that philosophy and add it to mine and continue on in my life.' I want to be good, and I want the world to be good. I want to share happiness and goodness with everyone. No one needs to be depressed. You know, like when the band broke up, I was hurt. When Eddie called me up and said, 'Man, you frustrated me so bad, I went and got David Lee Roth back in the band. We've been working together and it's going great. You might as well go back to being a solo artist. You don't listen to anybody. You've always acted like a solo artist, you might as well go back to being one.' I was like, 'What?' I was so ... I was angry. I jumped up out of bed, and I was ready to kill. 'David Lee Roth? He was the enemy,' I thought. You know, 'He's singing through my microphone, and I'm sitting here changing my baby's diapers.' I was (expletive). When that happens, there are two things you can do. You can either crawl into a hole and be wounded, and be less of a confident human being and let it beat you down. Or, you can go, 'I learned something from that. I'm a wiser person right now, and I'm a smarter person, and that will never happen to me again, because I'm wiser than that.' Therefore, I'm a bigger person. I'm a more confident person. And I can walk around saying, 'Hey, I just got hurt by that, and now I'm stronger.' And that's the way I do things, and that's the way I would like to address that to the whole world, because that is really important. Everything that happens that hurts, it makes you more strong, and it makes you a wiser person, more intelligent, and therefore, you should have more confidence about yourself. Now, it's, 'I'm smarter now. I should've seen that; now I see that, and now I know.' All those things can make you stronger, not weaker. That's the Sammy Hagar philosophy in a nutshell."

Yeah, it's good to see you walking in that. Well, what do you think of Jesus Christ?

SH: "Man! (laughs) What do you say about that? I think that if what we are reading today is held true to His philosophy, then He's one of the greatest men that ever walked the earth. You can't say anything bad about a person like that. Anyone that was unselfish, and anyone that was willing to take the pain Himself so that you didn't have to suffer, to me, I know that's Christ's consciousness, but no matter where that came from, I would still say that is a great thing, you know, a godly kind of thing. That's what I think about Jesus Christ. The organizations that are built around Christianity right now, most of the time, make me sick. You know, the Bakkers and the Swaggarts, and there's a lot worse ones than those, but those are just the ones that have been exposed. I'm not saying that is Christianity. And that's not Jesus Christ's fault. It's man's fault. I think that it's been exploited and crutched and leaned on, and that part of it makes me sick, so it keeps me from saying, 'Yes, I am a Christian.' But other than that, I am a Christian. In my heart, completely. I believe that in the philosophies, it's the way to live life. I think it's one of the great religions of all time, but there are other religions. You can't just be confined to Christianity, like some organized Christian churches say, 'You come to this church; you can't go to another church.' That is wrong. That's like, 'Hold it now. You can't go to another church?' (expletive) You can do anything you want, as long as you don't hurt another person, you don't inflict your power on a person, you don't try to do evil to another person. There are certain rules you follow, and you can walk into any church, you know. Hinduism, and all those things, they have a lot to offer as well. All those men are like Jesus. They were a different avenue to God, and I do not believe that Christianity is the only avenue to God. I just don't believe that. I believe you can be born onto this planet and be enlightened and understand God from birth, and never even hear the words 'Jesus' or 'Buddha.' You could still understand God. There's a lot of different ways. That's the only thing I have about the organizations. Other than that, I probably am more of a Christian. And I'm a rebel too, (expletive)!" (laughs)

And a redheaded one at that!

SH: "Well, I'm semi-blonde. Red is my favorite color, as far as that goes. I like the power of red."

What do you think about the claims of Christ to be the Way, the Truth and the Life—"No one comes to the Father but by Me?"

SH: "I think that's something that man made up—I'm not sure, though. I can't say in my heart that I believe that, but I also can't say that I know for a fact that it's wrong. I just don't think that ... I think it's just been misinterpreted and taken out of context. You're a journalist. You've done interviews. I'm an artist that has done interviews, and I've read things that are taken out of context, and they don't mean at all what I've said—just because they've been taken out of context. I really interpret that as Christ saying, 'My beliefs ... my beliefs,' you know, 'The way I preach life, is you don't hurt another, you don't kill ...' You know, The Ten Commandments. Let's use those for the example. I believe that He's saying, 'This is the way to God.' You don't have to go through Him, and use Him, like He's saying, 'I'm the egotist,' or 'I'm the vehicle.' He's teaching. If you don't obey these rules, you will not go to heaven, and not be in touch with God.' But there's other rules as well, and I don't think, like, if you learn those rules, true ... you yourself, if you taught me those rules, and I learned 'em, and I lived 'em, then I can do it. I don't think Jesus was doing it as an ego, power trip thing, like, 'I'm Jesus Christ, you have to come to My house first, you have to go along with My program, and then you get to go.' I think He's saying, 'These are the rules.' He presented them, and I think they've been taken out of context, for the organized Christianity people to say, 'You have to believe in this, and

you have to do this, and you have to send us money, you have to support us.'
It's become big, big business, and you know it. And I think it's been misinterpreted over the years. If I could read Sanskrit, then I could find out the
true meaning of that. But, you know, through interpretations, and all that, I
think too much pressure has been put on Jesus Christ, the Man, Who did His
duties to this planet, to bring people closer to God. I think too much emphasis has been put on Him, rather than His teachings. His teachings are what
we need to learn. And if we learned 'em ... I mean, I don't care if you learned
'em through the devil! Those teachings are what are important. Some people
learn from bad experiences. Some people learn from screwing up so bad that
they hit bottom. You know what I mean? Like, a drunk, or a drug addict, or
a killer, and then they go, 'Wow!' and it finally dawns on 'em. Well, drugs,
you know, or a weapon that would take another person's life, that's the worst
thing you could possibly do. That's the devil's work, but if it brings you to
the reality of Christ's teachings, hey, you're there, man. Even Christ said
that: forgiveness, right? You're cool. I think too much emphasis on the Man
Himself, and if He were walking around here today, He would go, 'Hey man,
don't be looking at Me. I can't save your (expletive). Only you can save your
(expletive).' And He made it pretty easy on us. Those rules are so simple,
The Ten Commandments. I mean, humans are so stupid that they had to
finally simplify it. Just don't use God's name in vain. I mean, how simple is
that? Okay. Don't kill someone. Okay. Don't screw your neighbor's wife.
Okay. It's just really simple, man. Anybody in their right mind could live by
those rules. I think that's all Christ was really trying to do."

I can respect that ... I think He was, like, a servant to the max. Like, the
night of the Last Supper, He took off all His clothes, He wrapped a towel
around Himself, and He washed their feet. And then He took the towel off
and dried their feet. And that's the epitome of humility. But I come to the
conclusion that the reason He died is because of His claims, that He claimed
to be God. To a Jewish culture, you don't go around saying, "I am," and
"Before Abraham was born, I am," and "The Father and I are One." I mean,
He knew what He was getting into, in the context of the people He was
talking to. And so, in my opinion, He went to His own death, not for His
teachings, but because of Who He said He was, and that He was the sacrifice
that's gonna take the pain, like you said, for us, so we don't have to. But to
me, there's a lot of common ground between every religion in the world,

when it comes to the exterior parts, like, "Be nice to each other." But when you get to the core, you've got one in Buddhism that says, "Become nothing, and just isolate yourself from everything." And then you've got Christ, who said, "Serve mankind," and "I am God, and I'm dying for your sins, and you can get forgiveness ..." The closer you get to the middle, the more you find that they don't agree with each other.

SH: "I think you're right on the money. I agree with you 100 percent. But the difference is, let's say you've got Eastern people, like, you know, the Buddhist philosophy. You've got that consciousness, that lifestyle. Buddha was the man to relate to those people, and could take them there. That's why I say there's different teachers, and the important thing is that you get to a godliness through an enlightened faith. It doesn't matter how you get there. See, Jesus related to His people, and it's just like every disciple that came from these different areas, they had to have their qualities. It's like me, mister blonde, curly-haired white dude ain't gonna go down into the ghettos and grab these black crack people, these dealers, and people that are out there killing people in the street, these gang members, and go, 'Hey you guys. Knock it off!' That ain't gonna work. You need some other black dudes that are just like 'em, who finally come up one night, and go, 'No, no, no, this is bad (expletive). Put your gun away.' And they go, 'Who the (expletive) are you, man?' 'Well, it's me.' That's what it takes to deal with those kind of people. That's why I'm telling you why Buddha was right for his people, and for that area, and Jesus was right for His. And now, we've grown up into a world that now, we can get on the telephone and talk to someone in Israel or China. Therefore, now Jesus is international, and Buddha is international. But at the time, they were just neighborhoods. Well, they were a little bigger than that, but you see what I'm saying. Of course, they sort of disagree, and that's where man has misinterpreted their writings and teachings. Because really Buddha is saying that, 'In order to live a Christ-like existence, such as pure, giving love, I have to go to the mountain, because in my world, if I wash people's feet and stuff, I'm a peasant. Some guy's gonna ... I'm gonna make that guy be a bad guy, because he's gonna take advantage of me and make me his servant.' Because that's the way they have it there. They're servants. So in order to break all those rules, you have to go up into the mountains, and you have to hide away to become enlightened so that you don't influence anyone to be a bad person. So it's half your fault if someone (expletive) up around you.

"So, Christianity is a great philosophy, but you go out and, say you're walking down a cobblestone street, and your feet hurt and you're barefooted. Well, Christ would say—I don't think Christ would say this, but—well, the philosophy would be that you take all the cows, kill them, take their hides, and cover the whole road with them so that we can all walk, so it won't hurt our feet. And Buddha would say, 'No, you take a piece of the cow, and you'd wrap your individual feet.' You know what I'm saying? That's kind of like, 'You take care of yourself, and if you're perfect, the whole world's perfect.' Christ is saying, 'No, the whole world has to be perfect first.' And it works either way. If everyone was like you, then they'd be perfect, and the whole world would be perfect. But Christianity is more like, 'Help your brother,' and I like that. That's why I say I'm more of a Christian, but I can see the philosophy of an Eastern person. You had to be an individual, you had no choice. Genghis Khan, man, if you come around saying you want to wash his feet, he'd say, 'Yeah, well, I'm cuttin' your (expletive) head off.' But you walk your (expletive) down to the ghetto, man, to a crack house, all those crack dealers with guns and some (expletive). You go down there as some white dude, man, it ain't gonna work. You need Martin Luther King to go down there, at best. That's the way I look at it."

That's a good point. I still don't buy into the fact that they're telling the same story, because Jesus talks about a heaven and a Father, and Buddha talks about nothingness.

SH: "Yeah, I don't like that part of Buddhism. I must admit. I don't believe in that. Buddha is all for life, in a way, and I believe life is a wonderful, wonderful thing. But those guys are so much heavier and deeper than us, that you can't quite comprehend what they're talking about. That one baffles me, because I'm not anti-life. I'm pro-life. Life is so cool. I'm the opposite of that."

Hey, do you have a cousin named Ken Tamplin, who's into Christian rock music?

SH: "Yeah, but I've only met him once. But you know, he sends me his records and all that stuff. Yeah, he's totally into Christian stuff, which is cool. There's nothing wrong with it. I just think it's been so abused. I would almost be embarrassed to say I would have belonged to one of those organizations. The Bakkers, I think, and the Swaggarts are the worst in my mind. But those are only the big guys that they've exploited. You don't how much of that (expletive) is going on everywhere. I've seen it too much. But, like I said, you can't blame Jesus for that."

Right, I think it's interesting that no matter where you go, you tell those stories about Swaggart, and everybody gets mad, because I think everybody has a sense of justice. You know, it's just not right to be a hypocrite.

SH: "It's not right to use God's or Jesus' name, power, or anything, for your personal gain, or pervert—much less, in a perverted sense—in an evil sense. To me, that's more like the devil than anything. That's the devil rearing his ugly head right there in those people, because that is evil. That's much worse than a crack dealer, in a way. In my heart, I want to always be good. I want to be godly. I want to project that, but it keeps me never trusting anybody.

"What the (expletive) are you trying to do to me? Make me think!? (laughs) This was kind of a refreshing interview, instead of just talking trash, you know."

[Originally printed in July/August '97 Issue #66]

"Those who really believe in Him really don't question the existence."

—Jerry "Only" Caiafa

photo by Frank White

The Misfits are one of the seminal bands of the '70s and '80s punk rock scene. Listen in on this HM exclusive as Doug Van Pelt speaks with Jerry "Only" Caiafa about the band's place in the music world, the comeback record (American Psycho), and, uh ... faith in Christ? [Note: As this chapter is being edited for this book, I look over my shoulder at the Jerry Only doll that I purchased last weekend at a toy shop. Point being, this is certainly a seminal rock band. They had dolls made, for crying out loud!]

Well, how did the recording of *American Psycho* go for ya?

JC: "It went very smooth. We were very prepared for it, which, we felt real confident going into it. We were a little anxious in the beginning, because Doyle couldn't get the guitar sound he wanted, but me and Doc were up and ready to go, so we dropped the whole album in two days. And then we had to stand around and wait for everybody else to do everything, and we were just like, 'Oh man …!' It's so hard to wait, you just want to play every day."

Well, a lot of punks really look down on the whole pompous rock star thing in the late '70s. I don't remember who it was—I want to say the Damned, but I don't think it was them, because Zeppelin was into them—but they said, "Whenever I look at a Led Zeppelin album cover, it just makes me want to puke." And now that punk is popular, there are punks in punk bands that look to bands like the Misfits as icons of punk culture. How do you feel about the tables being turned, now that you're admired alongside bands such as Aerosmith and Led Zeppelin, and what have you?

JC: "Well, that's really great. I mean, that's—when I was a kid—where I always wanted to be, so it's nice to be in that category. That's what I always say. Like, in the top five bands … We'll probably be in the top five bands of all time if we can do a good job from here on in. So when people come up to me and say, 'Oh, you guys are one of the best bands of all time,' I'd say, 'Look, what we're trying to do here is to make bigger and better music than we ever did, and really judge us from today on, not so much what we did twenty years ago.' I mean, it was great, but at the same time, it was when it was, and it was great music to listen to, and it's great to be able to go out there and have seventy-five songs to choose from when we play a set, and you can't pick a loser, because I think every song is good. But it's really the fact that, I think, we've hung in there for so long, and that we still have something to offer. After twenty years of music, we can still come out and be fresh and new. And I think that says a lot for the type of music we play, and the style of music we play, and the way we approach each gig in such a matter. It's always a big event for us to go out and do a gig, and we try and prepare as much as we can. And this new album, I think it's our best. And yeah, everybody says, 'Well, you've gotta say that, it's your new album,' but at the same time, I think it's … I've never worked harder on anything. Each guy that listens to it in the band, probably likes 90 percent of it, and then 10 percent of it drives him up the wall. But another guy's 10 percent winds up being totally different. Not everybody hates the same thing. It's like, I'll hate something, and Mike will like it. He'll like something he did, and I'll think that thing stinks, that part, you know? So it's a real team effort. I think it's a strong comeback for this band, and a real strong first step back into the music business."

What's the most exciting thing about performing live for you?

JC: "The kids."

What part of the show do you like the best?

JC: "I like the whole thing. The scariest part is right before you go on, and the end is always good, because I usually get to go out and meet all the kids and say hello to everybody. So I enjoy that. And it's really neat to see how much they enjoy it, because I enjoy doing it. I would do it if there was nobody there, but when you got a whole bunch of people in a room, and they're just going crazy, it just makes you want to do it even more, and when you do it, it's like you can suck their energy in and just keep going without getting tired. That's when you know you're really coming across, and people are liking what you're doing, because it's the feeling too, when you come see us. It's not just something you listen to, something you enjoy. It gives you a feeling inside. It's good."

Cool. What's the weirdest thing you've ever seen at a show?

JC: "Wow ... Uh, I'll tell you what. I think the weirdest thing is when things go wrong at a show, and things start getting violent and stuff. Things go into slow motion. I think that's the weirdest thing about the situation, when somebody's, like, getting into a fight, or getting into an argument. And when we play, it feels to me, like between songs, we take an eternity. Then I sit back and watch the tapes, and we're, like, going from one song into another. For me, I just want to get there so much sooner. For example, we were in Europe last summer, and this giant kid—he was just a giant kid—he stepped up on the stage, and he was real drunk, and he was swingin' over, messing with Doyle, and, like, hand signaling, 'Let me play your guitar.' And he was just real sloppy drunk, like barely able to stand. And Doyle just stops playing, looks at him, and gives him this two-handed shove, like, 'Get the hell outta here.' And the dude just kinda leaned back, and then, like, grabbed Doyle, and then they both fell into the crowd—it was in slow motion. It was the weirdest thing. I was like, 'Nooooooo ... waaaayyyyy ...' They just blended into the crowd, and they were so big, the two of 'em together, that the crowd couldn't absorb that much mass, so they kinda like sat on the top of the people's heads, and then slowly sunk like the Titanic. It was pretty crazy. And then we had to go get him, and then played another song."

What are your favorite places to play?

JC: "I like New York. I like Chicago a lot. Detroit's getting a little bit violent. I used to like playing there, but they hurt my fans, and I've got a problem with people hurting my people. So L.A. is always good for us. Texas has been good. Florida just wound up being really good for us. House of Blues, is my, if I had to pick one place to play, I would say the House of Blues places are the best. They've got the best lights, they got the best hospitality, they feed you, they help you with anything you need. You don't need anything when you're there. They make sure you get hooked up. And they've got them all over the country. We played one in Disney, in Orlando, that was, like, so cool, and actually, across the street from it is this giant Virgin Megastore. And so, what happened is, like, the girl who was in charge of doing promotional stuff happens to be from New Jersey, so we started talking to her, and the next time we go down there, we're gonna do this big in-store autograph signing at this giant Virgin mega-store, and have a gig right across the street, so we're thinking about setting up barbecues and doing hot dogs and hamburgers and stuff."

Right on. What are some of the highlights of your career?

JC: "I think, seeing a lot of great musicians, like John Sunders, I got to see. I got to see The Jam when they first came to the United States. I got to see the Clash when they first came here. When you go to a country like the United States, and you're from another country, you know you've got to put out, especially the first time you come, because you're real psyched about goin'. I know I am, like, when we went to Japan, I was so psyched to play Tokyo. And I think that when bands come here from Europe or from Japan, or wherever they come from, and they play New York City, they are playing the hardest that they've ever played in their life, and I got to see all these shows. It was fun growing up in this scene when it first came out."

I bet it was.

JC: "Yeah. It was intimate. It's kinda like it is now. It hasn't changed."

What do you think of Jesus?

JC: "Good friend of mine ... my boss, actually."

Alright. What do you think of His claims to be the "The Way, the Truth, and the Life, no one comes to the Father but by Me?"

JC: "I think that's pretty accurate. I know how I feel about my kids, so I'm sure if I had to give 'em up for somebody, they'd better have a good reason to come back."

Is there anything about Jesus that you hate?

JC: "No. I don't think you really could. I think that's the whole point of the figure, is that, you know, 'What are you gonna say?' And then at the end, He took a lump. You know, anybody can get screwed on this planet. You gotta deal with it. And I think that's a lot of the message too, you know?"

What is the most profound thing about His life or His teaching in your life?

JC: "Well, I just think it's the feeling, once again. I think it's something that you know inside, and you know, those who really believe in Him really don't question the existence, and you know why you're here, and things come to you one at a time. So everything that comes to you in your life, you gotta handle it in some kind of fashion, and I think what it does, is it gives you an angle of how you should perceive things, and what should be done to make it a better place. I think that's a lot of just the feeling in it, and I think it's something you carry it around with you every day. So it's a matter of how hard you want to carry it, and you know, I live that way. I try and do whatever I can for anybody, but at the same time, I don't appreciate getting screwed. That's just not the way things should be, you know? And I think that's pretty much the bottom line. So until you screw me, I'm your friend."

How do you deal with forgiveness when you get screwed?

JC: "Well, it's easy. I think that's just a true lesson. You've gotta be bigger than your problems."

How does your belief in Christ fit in with your career in the Misfits?

JC: "Well, I think the Misfits is a very classy act organization, and I think that everybody that's here handles themselves in a very polite, hospitable manner. And I think that's one of the good vibes about the band, is that it's got a very positive energy to it. And I think it's all based upon just the way you live with it, which is pretty much what you believe."

Have you ever heard of some of the Christian punk bands, like the Crucified?

JC: "No, I haven't heard of those type of bands. I really don't get involved in that aspect. I'll tell you the truth, I'd like to take my family to church a lot more than I do, and I'm hoping that once I've got a little more time, and I don't have my back so much up against the wall with trying to launch this thing, then I can sit back and enjoy what I've got, instead of having to go out there and kill every day to keep it. It's gonna be much more of a religious kind of an atmosphere, I think, in my life. And I want to learn how to play keyboards too. And so, if I could learn, I would play at the church on Sunday, just to stay practiced."

What's the last ten years of your life been like?

JC: "A lot of hard work. That's it ... and different things. I could go into a list of things that we do ..."

In your opinion, what is the most undeserving band out there today, and why?

JC: "Probably the Sex Pistols, just because they didn't do anything different than they did that long ago. And they tell you they're stealing your money, and they still get it."

I noticed the Misfits logo is trademarked. Why is that, and what kind of problems have you had?

JC: "Well, you get problems from everybody, and then you get people who bootleg your stuff too. So it's more of a protection than it is a remedy."

Well, what are your plans for the next couple years?

JC: "Exactly what I'm doing."

Well, have you ever played with another band that you had to fight with?

JC: "No, I think most bands are very cautious around us in the beginning, and they don't really know how to take us. But if you're around us more than one day, it's easy to get along with us. We try and work out the situations that arise. And really, that's what you need to do. And a lot of times, you've got to play the hand you got dealt, and you just gotta deal with it. And sometimes, for example, you don't get sound checks, or you get equipment that doesn't work, that's supposed to work, when you go into a venue. And you can get aggravated about it and be a jerk to everybody, or you can just say, 'Oh well, let's get through this,' and help everybody else get through it at the same time. A lot of people look at us just to get the whole vibe of the tour and how things are gonna go, and we've got a very efficient crew, and we play with bands that are much larger than us. We come out with, like, a green beret team, and just do a giant job with a minimal amount of people. And based upon that, they know, 'How are these guys gonna handle the situation? They obviously have their (expletive) together. How are they gonna conduct their lives?' And when something goes wrong, we try not to yell at each other in front of anybody. You'll never hear us raise our voice to each other, and it's a very constructive atmosphere that we try to transmit, and we work through problems together. If the sound man's got a rough problem with the PA, and I've gotta turn my amp down, I don't pull any rock star (expletive) and say, 'Oh, I'm not turnin' down ...' I accommodate him. And I tell the people, I'll say, 'Look, I'm sorry. I brought ten amps, and I can only turn on two. I apologize.' I've found I've had to apologize about equipment all the time, playing the kind of clubs we play. But we play these clubs, because otherwise, they're not gonna see you. And I think that we're something that you gotta really see it to believe it. Have you seen us play, or not?"

No, I don't think I ever have.

JC: "Where you from?"

Austin, Texas.

JC: "Okay, we were just down there. You just missed us."

I know you've been here before.

JC: "Yeah, so you're definitely gonna have to check it out. That's an opinion that I'd like to see."

I'd like to check it out, and maybe hang out with you after the show.

JC: "Oh, for sure!"

How would you describe the typical Misfits fan ... well, not the typical, but the hardcore Misfits fan?

JC: "Misfits fans are very loyal, and I think that what you find out is that they really love the band. They love the band just because of the way the band is, and they don't try and change you or mold you into anything. They're very accepting of the way you are, and they're very supportive. I think we've got just about the loyal-est fans out there, and we try and treat 'em good, so in return it's a very good situation we have."

What are your feelings about the person of Satan?

JC: "Well, that's not really my battle, unless it comes to my front door, so

I'm ready for it when it comes, but I don't really have an opinion. I guess that with light, you gotta have dark, and that's the bottom line. I think it's a balance thing. It's always there, it always will be. So I think it's each person's individual thing to try and deal with it."

Sounds like a pretty healthy attitude, instead of trying to go out and go up against something.

JC: "Well, no, you're into handling, and you find that a lot of things you do shape a lot of what other people do, so it's important that you do what you can. And sometimes you gotta go out on a limb, and sometimes, you know, you look at a situation, and you help somebody out, and you wound up takin' it in the back. But then again, you find a way to absorb it and keep going, and somehow you kind of help them out."

Any advice to young bands getting started today?

JC: "Yeah, 'Stay in school.' When I started the band, I was seventeen coming out of high school, and I blew off school to play in the band. And as a result, I didn't get an education. And when I look back on it, I could've spent those four years in school. I probably could've did the gigs that I did, and still made both things work, and I didn't do that. So that's something you gotta ride through. And another thing is, it takes a lot of money. Right now, we're trying to start our own label, which we're in the process of doing. And things take a lot of money, and it takes a lot of equipment, and you've got to really be in a responsible situation. You got to be able to have a credit card with you when you travel, and things like that, and people to back you up on the home front too, so you know, anybody that thinks they're gonna be an island, without capital to really make the job go, is out of their mind, so you've got to hold a steady job to pay your bills while you're in the band."

What kind of bands are you looking at signing with your label?

JC: "Right now, none, until they come to me, and say, 'Look, you have a problem. You have X amount of money, and you can either pay tax on it or spend it on a band,' and I'll help a band, but until I can help a band, until I get to that point, it really is not something I can do, because I wouldn't sign a band and not have the means to do the job right for them. That would be, like, really hurting them, and I wouldn't do that to somebody. Either I do the job for you and do it right, or I ain't gonna do the job at all. I've been through that end of it, too."

Cool. Any other parting comments?

JC: "Uh, no. I think you pretty much covered it. The school one is usually the one I add."

Yup, that's good advice. Well, I hope to see you next time you're in Austin, or if I'm ever in a city you're playing at.

JC: "We run in Austin, so you'll get to see us."

[Originally printed in July/August '98 Issue #72]

"Everybody
is different,
and you
can believe
what you want
to believe."

—Tommy Stewart

GODSMACK

7

This *"So & So Says"* feature brought a fast-rising metal star known as Godsmack to readers' attention. An unknown indie band from Boston just a little more than a year before this interview in 1999, this band was a true "indie underdog does good" story. After playing out regionally for a while, this quartet recorded and pressed their own album. A local radio station invited them to be on a compilation CD, they recorded the song "Whatever," it was picked up by a DJ, who started playing it on the radio, and then the DIY ethic exploded for them. One indie record store alone was selling something like eight hundred to one thousand units of their custom CD per week!

At this point, the radio airplay was spreading all over the country, and HM *editor Doug Van Pelt caught the band in Austin, Texas, during a stop on a nonstop tour that included a performance on* Late Night With Conan O'Brien, *and continued through the Ozzfest that summer. Scheduled to interview Sully, the lead vocalist, who unfortunately was sick, he talked to Tony Rombola, the guitarist, and Robbie Merrill, the bassist, instead. This interview, like the dreaded Korn interview ruined by Danzig's soundcheck, was partly muffled by a local band checking, so he had another chance for a phone interview with Sully, but Tommy Stewart the drummer came on the line instead. I guess an* HM *interview with a Wiccan disciple was not to be ... Read on as three-fourths of Godsmack answer questions on God, music, and the questions themselves.*

How did you guys hook up with (manager) Paul Geary (from Extreme)?

TR: "Sully knew him before. He used to be in a band called Strip Mind. He was signed and everything. He toured and the whole bit. He's a really good drummer. He played all the drums on the CD. So, being a drummer, that's how he knew Paul."

Congrats on the Ozzfest gig.

TR: "It's going to be really cool to play with the original Sabbath lineup. It's huge for me, because that's one of the first bands I got into."

TS: "We're all very excited, obviously. I mean, who would have thought in 1999 we'd be able to see Black Sabbath together, you know what I mean?"

What are your other influences on guitar?

TR: "Oh, anyone. I've been playing for a while, so, I mean ... Jimi Hendrix, Jimmy Page, Jerry Cantrell. A lot of the new bands. I went through all the '80s shred guitars—Joe Satriani and all those guys, Steve Vai, Greg Howe. I just love little bits and pieces of different people. It goes full circle to the basics of Black Sabbath, where I started."

Now, Tommy the drummer was in Lillian Axe. Did all four of you guys come from the glam metal scene?

TR: "No. Sully and Tommy are. Me, I'm not. I was a carpenter my whole life. I just played guitar for a hobby. Robbie, the bass player, he played in cover bands and stuff. We worked too, for a living—a regular job. But those two (Sully and Tommy) were in bands and stuff prior to this band. I played in a cover band, but nothing really serious. This is actually the first original band I've been in."

What's your assessment of the whole music scene right now and the hard music ...

TR: "There's not a whole lot of it going on. (laughs) I can tell ya that, with all the hip-hop and rap being so big right now. Maybe that's why it seems to be going well for us—there's a big hole there. Soundgarden, Alice in Chains, all those bands are gone now, and maybe that's a void that we can fill, ya know? Not trying to say that we sound like any of those bands, but still there's those rock people just sitting around, waiting for something hard. Maybe that's why we're doing good. That's kind of where we're coming from."

How was the Conan O'Brien performance show for ya?

TS: "It was good, actually. It was kind of weird, you know, it's very strange, it's like, "1, 2, 3, GO ..." you know? We went through the song, like, three or four times, so they could do their camera blocking and audios, and stuff like that. We waited around for an hour 'cause they rehearsed some of the skits they were gonna do, so we were there from about two o'clock until about seven o'clock, and then we did our song, and then we left, 'cause we had to get on a plane and fly to Tampa. It was funny though, because we recorded the show in New York City, and we flew to Tampa 'cause we had to play there the next day, so we got to see the show in Tampa ... It was kind of weird—to record it in New York and watch it in Tampa."

Yeah, that's kind of trippy.

TS: "But we were all pretty happy with the way it came out."

So, what do you think about spiritual things?

RM: "I'm not really ... I stay out of it. I have my own little thing. I was never raised ... My father, he was a Catholic. My mother was an Episcopalian. I think it's a branch of Protestants. We never really ... they just left that alone. 'When you get older, you can do what you want to do,' kind of thing. I've always stayed away from it. I believe in your higher powers and stuff, but I'd never get into churches. I don't pray or anything like that. Um, it's like everybody in the band. They do their own little thing. Everybody stays out of each other's way with it. That's one thing I like about this band—is that you don't have to worry. Like, with Sully (being) into Wicca and stuff ... He doesn't really say anything about it. 'If you're interested, here's a book. Read it. See what you think.' The name (Godsmack) seems pretty nasty, but it has nothing to do with religion or anything like that. 'Instant Karma'— that's basically what we use it as."

So, you believe that there's something out there?

RM: "Yeah. There's something, ya know? I tend to shy away from it a little bit, and stay away. It's like ... I don't spend too much time thinking about that. I just get out, think positive, and treat people the way that I'd like to be treated, that kind of thing. I don't know ... When you see wars started over religion and that kind of stuff, you say, 'Why?' I just get it out of my mind. I don't understand it at all. You know, just 'cause you're a Muslim or because you're this or because you're that, you hate that person. Why? You don't know him. You don't know what he's about!"

I bet, even the religions that I don't even understand why they believe that, most religions, I think, probably get a bad rap on these wars, because ... I can't imagine anybody who really believes in anything—whatever—even if it's satanism, would want to go hurt somebody.

RM: "I'll give you one little thing. I deal with some depression in my life once in a while ... when I was younger. I was talking to my grandmother, and I said, 'I bet you're living in hell right now.' My grandmother said, 'You know something, your great grandmother taught me this. She said: 'You're living where you want to live. If you want it to be hell, it's hell. If you want it to be heaven, it's heaven; it's up to you." That's what made me change—to think positive all the time. If you hang around with negative people, you're gonna be down all the time. And you know, I keep that in my head all the time—'Hang out with positive people, think positive, and good things will come.' If you start thinking negative ... if you get into the negative stuff, you start getting a little down there. It's eventually gonna happen."

You can learn a lot from hanging out with people with gray hair.

RM: "Yep."

Well, what do you think of Jesus Christ?

TR: (laughs) "I don't know! I have no comment."

TS: "What do I think of Jesus Christ?"

Uh hum.

TS: "Oh, I remember the magazine that you write for. I don't know, I think that ... I have mixed feelings on that. I'm sure there's ... I'm not a very religious person, myself, and um, I'm not sure ... I wouldn't want to offend anyone. But I'm not sure what the relevance is to the band, you know what I mean? Is it because of the ... Is your magazine geared toward that kind of thing or ... ?"

Yeah, and we always deviate every issue and have an interview with somebody like Megadeth or King Diamond to Green Day ... to whoever ... and focus on, not just their music, but kind of their beliefs on spiritual things. It makes for pretty interesting reading, and for the artist, it's usually kind of different, because usually you're sittin' in the record company office doing the same old questions. You know, thirty minutes after thirty minutes of the same old questions. So, they're kind of different questions, and uh, a lot of artists kind of say, you know, "What's this have to do with my music?" Well, in some cases, nothing, but in other cases, everything—in the sense that, you know, who you are comes out in your music.

TS: "I don't disagree with you there. I just ... um, I mean, I have my own personal feelings, and they may not be the same as everyone in the band. I wouldn't want, in the words that I tell you, whatever they may be, to represent the band as a whole and give anybody the wrong impression about the band. You know what I mean?"

Well, so far, I've got two out of four of you guys answering the same question, so it might give a roundedness to the ...

TS: "Right. Well, I mean, speaking for myself, which is all I can speak for ... Um, 'What do I think about Jesus Christ?' I don't know. I guess I don't really ... I'm sure there's uh ... I mean, I thank God every day that we all have what we have, but I'm not like a ... I don't go to church. I just try to do right by people, so it gets done right by me. I don't really think about it too much, to be honest with you."

Uh-huh.

TS: "I think that's the basis of how I feel and how I live my life—treat people the way you want to be treated, and I think anything you're gonna send out in a negative fashion is gonna come back to you at some point. So, um, just be the best person you can be. I don't know how that relates to a supreme being as you might call it. I don't really think about that end of it."

I think on a real broad base, every religion in the world probably pretty much agrees on the philosophy of, you know, "Be nice to each other." It makes the world a better place. If you could boil down every religion to a common denominator, that would probably be it. You know, "Do unto others as you would have them do unto you—the golden rule."

TS: "Exactly."

But when you study different religions, like uh, Buddhist philosophy has the Law of Karma, where, if you do something negative, the negative's gonna come back around to ya. But if you take what Buddhism's really about, or you boil it down to, "Okay, what did the Buddha really teach?" He basically taught that the ultimate goal was to become nothing and to rid yourself of all flesh and physical ... you know, through meditation, become nothing ... There is no personal God; whereas Judaism, Christianity, and Islam say, "Well, there is a God." And then, of course, those three have distinctions between each other as to who's a prophet or who speaks for God and when did the speaking stop or start. Uh, so ... What do you think ... When you boil down Christianity, it kind of comes down to who Jesus said He was. You know, one of His quotes is, "I am the Way, the Truth and the Life; no one comes to the Father but by Me." What do you think of that quote?

TS: "Uh ... I don't know. Correct me if I'm wrong: An atheist doesn't believe in God, and an agnostic just doesn't know, right? Is that what it is?"

Right. Agnostic is kind of short for ignorant. Basically, it's saying, "I really don't know," whereas an atheist says, "Yeah, there is no God, period."

TS: "Um, I would never want to plead ignorance, but in this case, I guess I would be ignorant about the whole thing, because I didn't study it when I was growing up, and it hasn't really been a huge part of my life, to be honest with you. Like I said, I think I just live by the way of myself and try to do right by everyone and myself. I don't really put too much thought into it, and I think everything else in my life is pretty much gonna take care of itself. And that's, like I said, it's a touchy thing, because I wouldn't want to offend anyone or anyone to get the wrong impression of me or the band for that matter. 'Cause, to be honest with you, it's very sensitive. It's a very sensitive issue for a lot of people, as you can see ... People go to war over that kind of thing. And, like I said, I wouldn't want anyone to have a negative impression of the band or the individuals just because one person doesn't really think about it like someone else did. You know what I'm sayin'?"

Yeah.

TS: "I really don't know how else to say it to you, other than that."

TR: "I was raised a Christian, so I probably believed in all of it, but I'm confused sometimes. You have to really have faith. You don't know where to get it all the time. I don't go to church anymore. I used to follow my religion a lot better. I used to not stay away from it for so long. I used to wonder what's out there, but I don't really think about it much, I guess. I don't practice religion a whole lot. The only memory I have as a kid is going to CCD (Catechism of Christian Doctrine). Then my guitar ... I guess music has been my religion for a long time. Sully, on the other hand, is a completely different story. (laughs) I can't even speak for it."

RM: "I've never heard that before. Say that one more time?"

I'll just give you some of the context: He was a Jew, and He was talking to Jewish people, and the Jews believe there's one God, and if you make yourself out to be God, we're going to pick up stones to kill you, because then that's blasphemy, that's wrong. And He told them, these religious leaders, these Pharisees, "I am the Way, the Truth, and the Life; no one comes to the Father but by Me." Actually, they picked up stones at that point and tried to kill Him. [Editor's note: This context is wrong. He was actually talking to His disciples at this time.]

RM: "That's crazy. That's unbelievable. Man, I never really ... I don't really know what to say about that, 'cause I'm not ... I never got into it. So, you hit me with something I haven't thought about, and I'm trying to come back at you."

It's a pretty bold claim. One way you could look at it is, He's either lying, and He just told a lie. You can't call him "good teacher" anymore, because He lied. He's not a good teacher, He's a liar. Or He's a crazy guy, like you'd see in a looney bin. "I'm God!" Or He's telling the truth. I guess another aspect could be, "Well, whoever wrote this quote down was just making up a story." But, if the Bible's just a big PR scam, it does a pretty bad job of it. There's a lot of bad stuff in there that, if the Bible was trying to present a nice religion for the people, I would take out all this stuff that shows the disciples are stupid or somebody messed up, or Moses ...

RM: "Well, I think, all humans make mistakes—everybody! I don't care who you are. If there was a God, He made lots of mistakes. We all make

mistakes. I'll have to get into that. I've never really read it. I've been wanting to. I see it all the time. I see the Bible in the hotel rooms, and I'm sittin'
there doing nothing. I might, out of my curiosity, read it. It's funny too,
'cause my father was Catholic, and he was baptized and all that stuff. Not
baptized ... what's that thing you do?"

Confirmation?

RM: "Yeah. But he never, ever gave it any thought about his kids doing it.
He hated it. He was told he had to do it. He was forced. So, when it came to
us, it was never there. I went my own way. I was playing baseball and doing
this and doing that, and it never came in. Even up until my twenties, I was
too busy dealing with my own emotions and finding out who I was."

That's one thing I never understood about some churches—is when you look
at ... I've looked at some of the things they'll say in a Catholic church, like
for Confirmation. And these things are by the book, completely right out of
the Bible. I would say they're having people repeat the things that should
change their life and make them ... the light comes on, and they follow
Christ and walk with Him every day. But there's something the Church must
do ... They either make it boring, or they kinda make you feel like, "Okay,
you just do this every five days, and you'll be okay and go to heaven." They
kind of make it sound like a little compartment of your life. It seems like the
whole Confirmation thing should be like a life-changing moment for most
people, just because of the words they're saying. They're basically saying, "I
believe Jesus is Who He said He was. I'm going to follow Him." I guess,
somehow, the churches teach that you're just saying it and you don't really
mean it. I don't know. It's kinda weird.

RM: "I think people, when they're hurt or bummed out or something, that's
their way of relieving what's going on inside—to go into a church and pray
and hope. That's like their higher power. That's my view: They're basically
praying for themselves to get out of this bad mood they're in or whatever it
is—this crisis—and move on. That's how I look at the Church. That's what I
do with it. Now, I can do that without going to a church. I can just sit there
and have all these thoughts, just like I would be doing praying and doing
that. Everybody that goes to church, a lot of times, that's what they do. They

go in there because there's something wrong inside; they're not happy; there's a crisis; somebody might have died, or somebody's sick. They're hoping, they're praying that this person's gonna come around and get back to their normal self again."

That reminds me of a parable Jesus was telling. He was just teaching people, and He came upon these ten lepers. Leprosy, in those days, was really bad. They would have to stay in this colony, because it was contagious. And He healed all ten of them, and they're like, "Oh, Yeah, Yeah," and all go away. And only one of them came back and said, "Hey, thanks!" And He was like, "What happened to the other nine?" Only one of these guys came back and said thanks. That kinda reminds me of some people that come and they deal with that thing, but they move on.

RM: "That deals with respect too. They don't really respect anybody if they didn't come back to say thanks. That's what I do onstage, especially. A lot of times when we play, the monitor guy helps us out. I'll ask him his name and stuff. I'll say, 'Can you help me out? When I go over to that side of the stage, can you bring up my bass and when I leave?' I always make a point when I'm done, at the end of the show, to go by and say, 'Hey man, thanks a lot! I really appreciate it,' and I do. And if I forget to do that, I bum out. That's what it all comes down to, that respect thing."

I think it's really important for you and for me—and for anybody—if we're gonna talk about issues like this, is to treat each other with respect and, you know, be able to walk away with, "Okay, you think this and I think this. Well, we agree to disagree and, you know, have a great day."

TS: "Absolutely, absolutely."

And that's kind of what I want to do, is create a forum to be able to talk about some issues, not just this issue, but uh ... and, you know, treat you with dignity so you don't feel like, you know, "This Christian guy just thinks I'm a jerk because I don't believe in his God." Well, that wouldn't be very Christian of me to treat you that way.

TS: "Exactly, and that's kind of why ... I mean, I don't want to speak for anybody else ... but I think I grew up in the same way ... As far as being Catholic, I kind of grew up a little bit like that, and I think I saw all kinds of hypocrisies throughout history, and I didn't really care for that too much. But I think that's maybe why, over the course of my adulthood, that I just adopted, you know, 'Just try to do the best you can do by yourself and everybody else,' and that's really what the story is with me."

Do you ever think about how, if you start with the beliefs you were born with, the Catholic belief, that, "If there is a God, and He gave me a chance to live on this earth, that I should give something to Him or somehow try to find Him or live a life that is kind of giving back to Him what He gave me?" Do you relate to that, or have you ever thought about that?

TS: "Um, I can see where it's coming from. I guess I've never really thought about it that way. Not to seem selfish, on the other hand, as well. Yeah, I guess I never really ... I guess that makes sense to me, but I don't think that I live my life day-to-day with that in mind, you know?"

How do you feel about Sully kind of, not really being a preacher, but kind of subtly letting people know that he practices Wicca and has that belief?

TS: "I don't have a problem with it. I mean, um, I've studied a little bit about that religion myself, and it's very much like the things that I kind of live in my own life anyway. It's very karmic; it's basically about worshiping the power of the earth and, uh, it's not really about ... It's just about living. It's not really about, necessarily putting your faith in a Supreme Being, but it doesn't mean that he has this awful attitude about everything as well, so ... But it doesn't bother me at all; to each his own. Even in the same band, we could have completely different religious beliefs, and it wouldn't bother me at all, because that's your own personal thing, and uh, that's why ... that's what makes it so great—is everybody is different, and you can believe what you want to believe. You can say what you want to say at the end of the day. Like you said, even if we disagree, then as long as you have the respect of the person across the table from you, then, you know, you can go on."

Cool. If you wanted to label yourself an agnostic, how open do you think you would be to calling yourself a seeker or a seeker of truth?

TS: "Well, in that respect, I only said that because I was ignorant about one specific thing that you asked. Not that I'm ignorant and I don't want to learn anything, it's just that I was ignorant about what you were talking about. So, that doesn't mean that I said I don't want to get as much information as I can and be a seeker of truth necessarily. I mean, I don't know how much truth there is in this world, but, I mean, a seeker of truth as it relates to me ... You know what I mean? I guess that's about it."

How do you guys in the band in general—if you know how the band feels—how do you feel about the genre of Christian heavy music or bands like that?

TS: "Um, I don't ... To be honest with you ... I mean, I've heard Petra in my past, and I've heard Stryper ... I don't know how those bands are looked upon in the community like that, but I don't think any of us have any kind of uh ... You know, we don't really listen to that kind of music. I think that people have the right to use whatever form they can to... But I just don't necessarily like to be preached to in any kind of form, whether it be in that form, Christianity through music, or in something else. I just don't want to be preached to ... I just wanna ... But again, they're also telling about their own life experiences; that's fine. But I'm kind of straying from the question I guess, so um ... I guess we don't really listen to that kind of music or listen to those types of bands, so I wouldn't really know anything about that."

Yeah. I've got kind of a fictitious question that might not be totally relevant, but let's say Sully came up with a song that basically said something about, you know, worship your mother, uh you know, give reverence to the goddesses. Would you have a problem with that, would you consider that to be kind of preaching of a ...?

TS: "Uh ... worship your mother?"

Yeah. You know, the Wicca religion has a lot to do with the worship of nature and uh, stuff like that. So if there was a song that was really kind of perpetuating that belief or telling people to consider, you know, worshiping your mother or considering Wicca as a thought/belief system ...

TS: "Right. Well, I think if that was to happen ... Number one, I know that it would never happen, because, even though there are some things that he won't hide about himself, I don't think that he wants his own religious beliefs to be expressed in the band either ... That's his own personal thing. So, if that was to happen, I mean, I just think that you have to pick and choose your battles sometimes. Depending on what he was saying ... I mean, it all depends. That's a hard question to ask at this point, when it's completely ... it hasn't happened, or the actual circumstances aren't right in front of me."

Yeah, that's kind of what I meant. The name Godsmack kind of has a funny story behind it, and I think it's kind of a humorous thing, you know. "Hey look, God smacked you in the face, you know, 'cause you were dissin' on me."

TS: "That's what it is—instant karma."

Yep. How uh, have you ever heard God's character described as kind of a Fatherly and a loving character versus the whole smacking, vengeance ... you know, angry, priest kind of image that I think some religions teach?

TS: "Definitely. I don't ... I mean, those two words I think sound really good together. It's two words that you would never think about putting together that actually, as one word, I think are just kind of intriguing. I'm sure that they invoke all kinds of different things in different people. We're not trying to really shock anybody. It's just, uh, it's a word, you know, it's a name. Um, but yeah, I don't think that any one of us has the idea like there's gonna be repercussions ... I mean, we all understand that, you know, God loves everyone and all that kind of thing. We're not trying to say that, 'Watch your (expletive), otherwise you're gonna get hit for it!' It's nothing like that. It's just two words together that make up a whole different word, so ... Some things you really can't go too far into, you know? You take it for what it is, and you go on to the next thing. Don't take yourself too seriously is what I kind of live by."

Yeah, That's a pretty good adage, especially for rock 'n' roll.

TS: "Oh yeah, especially. Absolutely."

What are your thoughts on the resurrection of Christ? Like, if you look at today's date, 1999, it's based on the whole timetable of AD, the Year of Our Lord, and the impact that Jesus made to civilization. Have you ever taken a look at the evidence or somebody trying to argue whether or not He really rose from the dead?

TS: "Uh, to be honest with you, no I haven't. I haven't, uh ... I couldn't even comment on that, 'cause I don't know."

Well, I wish you guys the best.

TS: "Thank you very much."

And I'm glad things have turned out so well for you, especially being, you know, the underdogs that kind of make it big from their own hometown and everything.

TS: "Yeah, it's funny. When I was growin' up, I was always reading stories like this with bands—about how something happened really cool like this to a band. I always wondered about that, and it seems like the same thing's happened to us, which is great. I mean, we've all worked hard to get here, so it's not like an overnight thing, but it's a good story, you know. It's a very organic kind of story."

When you do think about it, do you ever think, "Well, someday I'll kinda get back to it?"

TR: "Well, I think deep down, I still do believe, because I still feel guilt when I do things wrong."

I was like that when I was younger, I kind of grew up in a church, and I thought, You know, I believe in the rapture and the second coming, and I thought, that'll probably happen in the late '80s, and I'll get right with God a couple years before that ...

TR: "Yeah, and try to cover everything up. 'Hey! You're supposed to forgive me!'"

When I kind of came back to God, I kind of felt like, well, I was just playin a game, because if He would've come back before I expected it ...

TR: "Well, I don't put thought into it, I guess ... I probably should ..."

Are you getting a lot of comparisons to Coal Chamber and/or Korn?

TS: "I haven't really heard any comparisons to Coal Chamber. If there have been any comparisons to Korn, I think it's probably only because they kind of paved a new way for themselves, and if a newer band has the same kind of ... even the same little stitch of sound, someone might say ... they might liken it to Korn, only because people are perpetually ... they constantly need something to compare something to. So, other than that, I don't think that the comparisons to Korn and Coal Chamber actually exist anyway, other than the fact that we may have the same genre of fans. We like Korn a lot. We listen to Korn all the time, so I'm sure they influence our music, you know, a little bit, but I wouldn't say that we sound like them, necessarily."

What sort of advice do you have for independent bands today? You've kind of been a really cool indie success story of how your band did it yourself. What kind of advice would you have?

TS: "Just basically, what happened here, which is, you don't have to move to the big city and then put yourself to be a small fish in the big pond. Just basically, get something on tape, record a CD if you can, and make as much noise as you can in your local area. That's exactly what happened to us. Um, and then, what people don't ... I don't think they realize is that all these record labels have these regional reps that look out for that kind of thing—to see who's had an impact on their area as a local band. And they scout these things. So, the best advice, I think, is to just stick it out and make some noise in your own area."

[Originally printed in July/August '99 Issue #78]

"You know, if you give Him a chance, He's gonna work through your heart, and He's gonna change your life."

—John Maurer

{ SOCIAL DISTORTION } 8

This issue's "What So & So Says" article began with a phone call to our mailing list manager, Chad Olson. Bass player John Maurer's wife called to get her husband a subscription to this magazine. In the conversation that ensued, it became known that John was a believer. Chad inquired as to whether or not her husband would be open to doing one of our "What So & So Says" features. She said he'd probably love it, and so the following interview took place.

JM: "So, what city are you guys in?"

Austin, Texas

JM: "Ooohhh. You guys have just got over the SXSW thing, huh?"

Yeah.

JM: "How was that? ... Crazy I hear."

Yeah. It was uh ... If you don't try to do too much it can be okay, so uh ... it was uh, kind of crazy ... It comes on the heels of a deadline for us, and uh ...

JM: "Right, it's like a carnival comes to town I kinda hear."

Right. Takes over the whole town. It's a pretty big festival. It's kind of fun.

JM: "Right. Right."

Okay, why don't you give me a brief history of Social Distortion.

JM: "Okay. My name is John Maurer. I'm in the band Social Distortion, as you know. Uh ... we started off ... the band started with its first couple singles, '1945' and uh, the first LP was called *Mommy's Little Monster*, 1982. I joined the band in January of '84 after a breakup because of personal conflicts that they were having. I've known Mike (Ness) and Dennis (Danell) since ... earlier than junior high school. That's how we knew each other ... being in the same scene. And we just have grown as a band ever since signing to CBS and Sony and uh, doin' our own record, and (it) just kinda grew from there ... to really turn into a lifetime career."

What do you think that people's general viewpoint of Social Distortion is?

JM: "Initially, if someone hasn't heard of Social Distortion, I think uh, the name really ... is almost offensive to some people. Um, I mean, 'Social Distortion, my word! Is that something?' You know, 'God, what is that? What is Social Distortion?' Well, it's kind of self-explanatory, you know. And it was a way ... a feeling that Michael got in the early '80s, late '70s. But, I think initially, people don't know what to think if they do know. You know, we have our fan base, and it's just kind of a big family that people know it as what it is, but you know uh ... hard to say."

What do you think Social Distortion is most notorious for? What are a few notorious events or things?

JM: "Um, within ... as far as being notorious, we are ... um, for being an early punk rock band, evolving into a rock band ... (we're) notorious for being sometimes out of control. We're notorious for being, uh, spiritual seekers in lyrical content."

What made you go indie, or DIY?

JM: "Necessity. Working with many bands in Orange County, and the L.A. areas ... [there are] a lot of fringe bands that I thought needed recognition that I would produce or do demos for. They just weren't getting ... no one was really paying attention to them. It's something I always wanted to do. Uh, I had some friends that are in a band, and, interesting enough, the name of this band is called Hellbound Hayride ... I've been doin' demos for them. We couldn't really get 'em a deal, and so we just kind of came to it where it was time to start Flip Records and go on from there ... and give them a platform to launch their music from. So that's kind of where that came from.

"So, I signed the band called Hellbound Hayride. [I] stuck in Romans 3:23 on their liner notes, which is kind of funny, but ... they ... I don't know, they had mixed emotions. They thought it was cool ... my big ministry, you know?"

Well, what do you think of Jesus?

JM: "I am ... this is a very special week for me. Uh, Good Friday, and Easter is more important to me than Christmas. A lot of people ... um ... in the secular world, want to celebrate Christmas, and I think they miss the whole idea of Easter, what it's about. I, myself, am a child of God. Um ... the work of Christ to me is very important. To be ... I strive to be Christlike, you know ... in my walk and um ... like I said, just striving and working on being Christlike."

What do you think about His claims to be, "'The Way, the Truth and the Life; no one comes to the Father but by Me'"?

JM: "Well, that's the absolute truth, isn't it? Um, that's freedom. You know, you go for life's pleasure ... and success, (they) aren't really gonna, you know, do anything for you. You know, self-reliance, having this ... going out with this huge trust in yourself and confidence in your trust is not really ... it's not freedom, although many people think it is. You know, running a successful band, a successful business through self-reliance isn't really gonna ... you know, and self-will and knowledge ... isn't really gonna get you that. You know, pleasure is the same thing. A feeling of satisfaction or enjoyment for a minute ... and even success will cloud the way of an absolute truth. You know, so just trying to get to some sort of state of being free, you know? I mean, you mention freedom, and people automatically think politically free or whatever, and they just kinda don't really understand, you know, liberty, or they don't really understand that you're true identity is Christlike. So, that's my strive, towards that freedom and always toward that.

"So, I mean, I totally relate to what you're saying. A relationship with God is the true identity. After all, we are modeled after Him, and He's our Creator. Hope I'm not gettin' too heavy for ya."

No, heavy's good; we used to be a heavy metal magazine anyway. So, what kind of challenges have you faced being a Christian in Social Distortion?

JM: "Um, I go through ... that's really mixed. Years ago I was a heavy drinker. In kind of a roundabout way, I found some spirituality through, um ... through a twelve-step program that ... by only one way of, 'Thy will, not mine,' you know? Meaning, 'Thy will of the Lord ...' Can you say that question again? I'm sorry."

What kind of challenges have you faced being a believer in Social Distortion?

JM: "Uh, I struggled with ... like I said, I went through a twelve-step program, and I found this ... you know, 'Thy will, not mine.' I wanted to research that more, because this enabled me to find spirituality and give this up to a higher being—as you know, kind of their basis."

Yeah.

JM: "And I'm saying, 'Well, man, this prayer stuff is heavy; this prayer works for me ... it took something away.' It took some chains off of me. In the beginning, I didn't want to do that. By being sober, I thought I was losing freedom. I was gonna lose the party, I was gonna lose my cool friends, you know? The party was gonna be gone. So, I thought I was releasing these chains, you know, and I looked at ... there's another thing, like, at the end of Matthew. I'm not really sure where it is, but it's about worry ... and ... not to worry, you know? But not storing our treasures here, but in heaven. You know what I mean? (I started) searching God—wanting to see what these were about—how He gets us through prayer. Going into Christianity, it's like: Now, all of a sudden, I have these chains again, you know? 'I'm gonna lose more freedom ... I gotta gain Christian rules and laws.' You know, 'Christians aren't fun. Christians can't have fun. I'll have to change the way I dress.' These are all lies, you know, that Satan was speaking to me. 'I'll have to pass judgment on friends, and you know, 'Pray?' You know, 'What are my friends gonna think?' That's weird. 'Christians are weird,' you know? But, the twelve-step program has a thing. 'I'm sick and tired of being sick and tired.' I got to the point where I got tired of tolerance, you know? I really didn't ... What I mean (by) tolerant ... you know, lifestyles that people live, um, my views on abortion, my views on drugs and alcohol, political views ... You know what I mean? For me to have a Christlike family value, I have to stand up to tolerance, and that was really tough for me, because I wanted to be, um ... I'm a 'bigot' now. I never was that 'bigot.' I was: 'Everybody has rights, everybody should be able to do what they want to do,' but I'm finding that, if I'm gonna live this lifestyle, you know, I can't be ... I gotta be tired of tolerance. (Through) the twelve-step program, I thought I was free of ... maybe just a link in the chain was broken. So now, through Christianity, I really can be free. And that's kind of a struggle. I don't have a problem with people, you know, because I just share my stories. The only answer that I have is absolute truth and stories that I can share with you ... and let Christ work in their hearts, and that'll change."

I think people have a false definition of the word tolerance. They think it means acceptance, but, like ... our bodies can tolerate so much poison at a certain point, like alcohol. At a certain point, alcohol becomes a poison that kills us. You have a tolerance level. You put up with it. And that's kind of what tolerance is. You put up with somebody who lies, steals, cheats, and is sexually immoral who lives next door to you. But you don't accept it, or you don't say, "I support that!" or, 'I put my stamp of approval on it." And I think that's what a lot of people think tolerance is—is approving other people's lifestyles in a way that's like, "Yeah, you can do it, it's okay."

JM: "Being tolerant, accepting that, saying, 'Yeah, well ...' And even being tolerant, saying, 'Yeah, I accept it, okay?' My neighbor is not like that. I mean, I'm not gonna go and I'm not gonna preach to someone about it. I'll speak with them if they ask me about it, and I'll share with them. It's a very touchy situation. You know, like I say, 'By me being tolerant, I'm becoming a bigot.' And that's a whole other can of worms, man. It's a very scary thought. But if I'm going to be truly Christlike, I have to go against this tolerance. I gotta stand up somewhere. I don't go around preaching these views, you know what I'm saying? But I'm just ... That, like I said, is a whole other can of worms."

Yeah. How do you deal with the whole expectation that gets put on you sometimes, where, "Oh, you're a Christian, you're born again? Then you have to go on TV and give your testimony, or you have to, when you get a chance to share with somebody, you gotta do it, or you're denying Christ?" Uh, "If you're in a band, you've gotta make it a Christian band now, or you've gotta leave because they're gonna sing about, you know, booze or sex, and you can't be a part of that!"

How do you deal with that whole expectation people will try to put on you?

JM: "Okay, how do I deal with being in a secular band ... and being a Christian, and what people's views are of me now, being a Christian in a secular band?"

Yeah, well, kind of a viewpoint of some people—who, maybe with good intentions, maybe not—a Christian who would try to say, "Now you're supposed to do this, this, and this, because this is how it's done." Kind of in the context of, "Okay, you're in a non-Christian band, or a secular band ... Now you're supposed to quit, or now you're supposed to preach." Uh, what are your feelings on that kind of expectation and all?

JM: "Um, believe me, Doug, I have struggled with this—especially in the beginning. I thought, 'Well, how could I be in this band? How could I go and put myself in the pit?' I'm going out into that pit every night. And I don't mean the dance pit. I mean, you know, I'm going out where the lowest of (the lowly) are. And I've struggled very hard with that, and it always comes to a point where it's like, I'm at my end. Um ... and then ... and I have people, they ask me these questions all the time: 'How can you do this?' Christians ask me. And then right when I'm about ready to just, you know, give it all up, someone will come up to me and say, 'Hey, tell me about that church, Rock Harbor, that you go to,' or 'I hear that Pastor Keith Page is a really cool dude. What's he like?' And that enables me to say, 'Come into our church,' you know, 'Everyone's welcome.' I mean, throughout my career, I had a ton of gay friends, I had a ton of drug-addict friends, I had a ton of just, people who are just, sinners. Well, I'm a sinner; we're all sinners."

Uh hum.

JM: "And, if a couple of them are coming to me asking me about my church, and coming ... most people just want to be asked to come to church, anyway. That's initially what it is. But, they're like, 'I'm gay.' It's like, 'Hey, come as you are, and let Christ ... let His love ... and it will work through your heart.' You know, if you give Him a chance, He's gonna work through your heart, and He's gonna change your life.'"

Yeah. That's pretty cool.

JM: "So, if I'm able to minister to one person of an entire tour, of an entire six weeks of going into the pit every night ... If I can pull one person out and change one person's mind ... You know, I'm not perfect. I'm a human being. I'm a sinner, and I'm gonna do that. But, if I could share what I know with one person, it makes it worth that to me. It's like the old saying, 'You don't go the doctor because you're well. You go there because you're sick.' Why should I just minister to Christians? You know what I'm sayin'?"

Yeah, absolutely.

JM: "We need to minister to people who need our help. And that's what

Christ did. He was down with the low of lowly. He wasn't hangin' out with the kings and pharaohs. He was in the trenches, man. He was with the common folk. He was with us. He was pulling out the tax collectors, the junkies, pimps, winos, and whores. And that's where I am. I'm with those people every night. I'm not gettin' too heavy here, am I?"

No, this is great. Um, what is your role in the band as far as lyrics, and album covers, and T-shirts, and stuff like that?

JM: "Mike Ness is the sole writer. He's is the idea man; Social Distortion is him from inception. Uh, it's all him. You know, I'm the bass player; I'm a friend. Uh, I'm there for him through thick and thin. I've known him for, gosh, twenty-five years, you know? That's a long time. So, we were young kids growing up. But, he writes all the (lyrics). He's a very spiritual man. He's a seeker. And I pray about him every night."

Have you guys played with any bands like MxPx or Undercover, or any Christian bands of the punk genre?

JM: "Um, we've played with MxPx in the past, but this was after when they signed to A&M, and they kind of ... I don't know, whatever it is, building their success, or whatever it is they were doing. Years ago, I ... before I got into the band, I was 'born again' for about a year with a very close friend of mine, Carla White, who happens to be a producer for Maranatha. A beautiful woman. I mean, she has a huge heart, you know? I started hangin' out with her, and we would go see Undercover. This was in the '80s ... and bands like The Lifters, you know, the rockabilly scene ... the Stray Cats were big then, so there was like a big rockabilly scene back then. Um, I was getting to another grand point here and I got sidetracked. I'm sorry, um ..."

Something about when you were born again. You mentioned like a year or something.

JM: "Oh, oh, oh! Okay, yeah, I'm sorry. And then I got into the band and, 'Bang! into the pit again' for a long, long, long time ... and doing all that false seeking I was talking about earlier, you know, self-reliance, pleasures, and seeking success, thinking I was gonna get freedom out of that."

Uh-huh.

JM: "You know, no way. It's not there. I'm blessed that I came around."

That's cool. So, what has your experience been touring with bands that are, maybe, really dark or people that are just totally lost? Do you have any interesting experiences about, you know, kind of a bass player or guitar player from another band talkin' to you and ...

JM: "Um ... People are strong. Satan's grasp is even stronger. Satan works on me every day. Satan works hardest on me Sunday morning when I'm tryin' to get up and go to church. I've dealt with some pretty dark people, and just by lettin' them know that 'Hey, I believe. I'm a believer,' and explaining that 'eternity's a long time ... and you better be right with yourself, and I hope you really know what you're doing.' When it gets down to it, usually I'll throw it out in a little jokingly way. You know, dropping little subtle hints, 'cause you can only bring the horse to water, bro."

Yeah.

JM: "You know what I mean? And it takes them to drink. And, just by throwing little pieces of this and that out, it's like putting the Romans 3:23 on the Hellbound Hayride *Sinner* record. You know, I'm just making an awareness. And that's really all I can do. And if I'm gonna get heavy about it, I'm gonna say, 'You better be prepared for eternity, 'cause eternity is a long time. A thousand years is but a day to the Lord. So, you better know what's up!' If someone really wants to come to me, and they're gonna start asking questions ... But I don't really like to preach."

Well, how can the readers of *HM* magazine pray for you?

JM: "Um, that my walk continues to grow. That my true identity continues to come through, and that I seek freedom from myself and everybody, and really just pray for the world."

What are some goals that you have before you?

JM: "Just kind of to, you know, to reach ... outreach. I would like to get, uh ... I'd like someday to work for a Christian label. I'm well into my thirties. I love Social Distortion, I'd love to play with them for years to come, and if so be it ... if that's the way it is, I will. But I would really like to work with Christian bands, young Christian bands ... putting together records for them. Maybe working for a Christian label would be really nice, you know?"

Okay, you're out in Orange County. What is really hot right now, music scene-wise? And, if different, what is gonna be the next big thing, or next bigger things, if there's more than one or two?

JM: "Boy, that's a good question, isn't it? Um, there's a saying in the secular industry, 'My crystal ball's no clearer than yours,' which is kind of hocus pocus, but it's true. No one really knows. The power pop thing seems to be real big in Orange County right now. The '70s New York punk vibe seems to be real big right now, which is my favorite kind of music. You know, I'm fortunate that my style of music has been able to come around through the Green Days, through the Offspring ... Some of my friends are really down on like, 'Oh, you can go buy Doc Martens at the mall now'; I think that's cool. I'd rather see that than, you know, doing spandex and you know, moccasins."

You used to be able to buy those at the mall too.

JM: "Yeah, exactly. You used to be able to buy that at the mall too. But it's like it's just kind of holding on ... I'd like to see more Christian hip-hop. I think there's a great ministry out there for that. Um, I think Christian music is gonna really come around in the future, only because I had an interesting conversation last year with some pretty high-up guys on the ladder at MCA, and these are Jewish men saying, 'Well, we're looking for Christian acts now, because, you know, that's what's gonna be big.'"

Whoa!

JM: "So, these are money men, so it's just ridiculous. But, let's hope so ... let's hope so."

Yeah, that'd be awesome to see...

JM: "I don't want it be ... get to the point where it becomes a fad ... a trend."

Right.

JM: "You know, I hope it stays true in people. So, mainstream's kinda bad. You know, you get up to the mainstream, and that just means there's someone down there right below on that ladder that's ready, just choppin' away at your stilt man."

That's true. Well, cool. So, you've been subscribing to *HM* for a while?

JM: "Yeah, a little while. My wife is, you know ... she's a key person in my walk. She's really, really strong in our family. So, not that long ... it's not really been around. But it's cool."

That's great.

[Originally printed in September/October '99 Issue #79]

"I will say that spirituality is definitely a part of my life. I guess music would be my religion."

—Troy Van Leeuwen

A PERFECT CIRCLE

{ 9

A Perfect Circle is definitely out there, turning some heads with their Mer de Noms *album, so we thought we'd give Gordon her first "What So & So Says" assignment, speaking with guitarist Troy Van Leeuwen on studio work, movies, touring, and Jesus ...*

First, I've gotta tell ya that I've just recently got into a band called Failure ...

TVL: "Ah!"

I take it you're familiar, huh?

TVL: "Oh, some history of me."

I know that Failure has had a lot of influence on a lot of music that's happening now. What influenced you when you were in Failure—you and Ken Andrews?

TVL: "Well, the funny thing is, and this is sort of a, you know, like a side note of my involvement in Failure, I only did one recording with them, and that was the cover of the Depeche Mode song, 'Enjoy the Silence.' I joined the band because I was a fan, and we were into a lot of the same things. They needed another guitar player, and I was available, so ..."

Did you perform mostly as their touring guitarist or ...

TVL: "Yeah, that was really what it ended up being, you know? I did join the band under the pretense that we'd be making another record, and I'd be involved in that, but that never happened. So ..."

Oh well, that's a bummer.

TVL: "Yeah, it was ..."

Now, were you involved in the mix with Replicants?

TVL: "No, that was also Ken Andrews and Greg Edwards ... with, you know, Paul Dumore and Chris Pittman."

Right, cool.

TVL: "A lot of that stuff was, you know, a lot of it was having fewer, um, influence and like Jesus Lizard and, and, you know, Pink Floyd, David Bowie—a lot of stuff like that. We shared the same sort of influences."

Very cool. Well, what has ... uh, how many live performances have you guys been doing so far?

TVL: "What? A Perfect Circle?"

Yeah.

TVL: "Boy, I don't know. This whole tour was like, is like, we're coming off ... In the last stretch of this tour, which has been like forty-eight shows ..."

Oh, my gosh.

TVL: "Plus, we did, like, a two-and-a-half week tour back in the fall and then a couple scattered gigs before that, so we're probably around sixty-seventy gigs."

Now, is this the one with Nine Inch Nails?

TVL: "Yeah."

How's that been going?

TVL: "It's been going really good. I mean, seeing a lot of new faces in the crowd and hopefully getting some fans along the way ..."

What's been the reaction so far of the audience?

TVL: "Really, really pleasantly good. Uh, really good responses. Yeah, I've no complaints."

Cool. Now, I know that you didn't record on this album, but have you done much studio recording?

TVL: "Well, actually I did play on two of the songs on this record ..."

Oh, okay.

TVL: "Uh, 'Sleeping Beauty' and 'Thinking of You ...' But, yeah, also I do a lot of studio work—a couple bands I work with, like Orgy, a band called Crazytown, a lot of stuff that isn't out yet that you'd be probably getting this summer."

Yeah, I hope so.

TVL: "A band called Dead Z, a band called The Start, a lot of stuff."

Which aspects do you like about live performance and studio recording?

TVL: "Well, I really enjoy the energy of the live performance ... Um, nothing beats it, you know? In the studio I like to just, you know, have pleasant mistakes, surprises. That's really where the magic is."

Yeah, um, how do you strike the balance between being, like, a sessions guy and being a band member?

TVL: "Well, (laughs) I don't know! I haven't really figured it out! (both laugh) I've been able to maintain it, not having to worry about it. I just try to make it work, you know? The studio is, really, you know, when I'm working with someone else or doing my own thing, it's really just easy to jump in and create, for me, anyways. It doesn't even really depend on who's involved. I'm always, like, the guy who can figure something out, you know? At the last minute if need be. But, um, I do like the balance, though. I wouldn't have one without the other, no way."

Good, that's good. How do you think people's perception will change, if it does at all, from looking at A Perfect Circle as Maynard's side project as opposed to seeing A Perfect Circle as its own entity?

TVL: "Well, I don't know. The reaction that we're getting, you know, in sales and radio and the crowds, I would assume that everybody that's coming to see us is under the impression that it is its own thing, which I think it is, just because, you know, everybody brings their own thing to the table at the same time as everybody's listening to each other. It really, really works well, because there's no real egos involved here, where somebody says, 'Oh, you know, I don't like that! Don't do that.' You know? Which, really, everybody trusts each other, and it's really [an] impressive unit actually, you know?"

Cool, that's awesome. Now, I've heard that most of the music was originally written by Billy Howerdel as sort of a film score? How has the translation from atmospheric to harder music come about?

TVL: "Well, I think that really had to do with the addition of each member. I mean, I write my own music too. And I know what he went through, like, you know, trying to get ideas down and, like, you have all these tools, and you really utilize everything, you know? At times you get really ambient, you know, textures when you're doing your own thing with a lot of the new Pro Tools and stuff for recording. I think that, uh, just adding each member really develops the sound for A Perfect Circle, you know, to what is now."

Cool, cool. So, uh, what are some names of, um, music, bands, musicians, whatever, that are influencing you or inspiring you these days? I know, before, you had mentioned The Cure and Pink Floyd and ... but what are ...

TVL: "I still listen to a lot of that. Recently, I've been going in and out of, you know, a lot of ambience stuff. Actually, I've been listening to a lot of the Cocteau Twins and This Mortal Coil, My Bloody Valentine, along with, like, Black Sabbath, The Cars. I like this project called Uncle, which is DJ Shadow and, like, a bunch of other artists."

You are very eclectic.

TVL: "Yeah, you know, we like to spread it out."

That's awesome ... so, uh, what do you think of Jesus Christ?

TVL: "What do I think of Jesus Christ?!"

Yeah.

TVL: "I think He was a cool dude. (laughs) I don't know how else to ... He was, like, a loner, a rebel."

Yeah? What do you think of His claim to be "The Way, The Truth, and The Life; no one comes to the Father but by Me?"

TVL: "Well, I think that ... gosh, that's a good question!"

Thanks! (both laugh)

TVL: "Um, I don't know. It takes some balls to say that, I'll say that. Um, I think, you know, my opinion of Jesus Christ is, you know, He was somebody with a passion about what He did, and, you know, people followed Him, and I think that what His name has turned into, as far as, like, how religion has turned out, I think, is just a farce, you know? I don't think ... I think that organized religion is really ... because, you know, people's way of saying, 'Okay, I'm not alone in this universe,' (I) think can explain it. Um, people need that, so it's valid for some people."

How about for you?

TVL: "For me, well, that's funny that you ask that, because I grew up in a very Christian environment, and I've come to the realization that a lot of what, uh, you know, religion has to say about, you know, reality and basic evolution of man goes against what I believe. That's what Darwin would say, you know? I don't think we were just thrown down here, you know? I mean, I appreciate the imagery and the, you know, the whole idea of paradise, you know—being lost, you know—but I don't know. I tend to be on the fence about it a lot, you know? Yeah."

I can understand how, you know, it's a tough question to answer, because there are so many people out there that are not giving Christians a good name, you know?

TVL: "That's what I'm saying, you know? It's like a lot of hypocrisy and a lot of double talk. It's a lot of ... hold on a second ... I'm sorry (phone rang), you there? Okay, uh, this phone just keeps ringing. Um, yeah, a lot of hypocrisy and a lot of, you know, I've definitely witnessed it, going to a Christian school and stuff like that. I just felt, like, you know, it was really a big popularity contest in the end, and I just didn't dig it. So, I do have a bad taste in my mouth about it, but I understand why it exists, you know?"

That's too bad!

TVL: "Yeah."

Your publicist said that you guys were going to be going on to Europe.

TVL: "Yeah, we are, yes."

Who are you going to be touring with over there?

TVL: "Well, we're kind of doing our own thing."

Oh, cool.

TVL: "Um, we're going to be doing a couple of festivals and some club dates. It's not really with any one band; we're just hitting a bunch of places."

Yeah, that's cool. So, what books are you reading right now?

TVL: "Um, gosh, I haven't picked up a book in a while ..."

You want me to leave that part out? (laughs)

TVL: "Yeah, actually I've been doing a lot of music, so it doesn't leave me lots of time to read. Um ..."

Do you have any favorite authors that, when you do get the chance to pick up a book ...

TVL: "There's some, you know, I do like—like Oscar Wilde, I like Nietzsche, I like Dr. Seuss."

Yeah! One of my childhood heroes.

TVL: "Yeah, me too. (phone interrupts again) Gosh, this phone will just not stop ringing, I'm sorry ..."

That's okay.

TVL: "Um, yeah, I'm trying to think ... there was a book by Nick Cave that came out a couple weeks ago called *And the Ass Saw the Angel*. I thought that was really interesting."

What was that about? Did you get a chance to read it, or ...

TVL: "Yeah, um, it's basically about, you know, he's from Australia, and it's about, sort of, like the real sticks area of what we would, like, probably call, you know, somewhere in the middle of Oklahoma, you know? Just about a mute that, you know, falls in love with this little girl, who he thinks is the angel, and it's really detailed and, like, the story ... it's just, it gives a pretty descriptive ... and there's a lot of twisted sort of imagery I kind of dig."

That's cool. So, have you had a chance to see any movies lately or ...

TVL: "What was the last movie I saw? Actually the last movie I went to go see was *Gladiator*, which I thought was okay. Before that, *American Psycho*, (which) I thought was really good ..."

Yeah?

TVL: "I like that one, yeah."

Cool, yeah. I haven't heard, like, raving things about *Gladiator* now ...

TVL: "Yeah, I mean it's a good sitting."

Alright, cool. Well, is there anything else that, uh, I may not have covered that you'd like to talk about?

TVL: "Um gosh, I don't know: 'Work hard and stay in school.' (both laugh) That would be my closing comments, I guess."

Yeah.

TVL: "What is *HM*? I'm not familiar."

It's hard … It stands for *Hard Music* right now, or some people say it stands for *Hard Music*. It used to stand for *Heaven's Metal* and, uh, we are a Christian hard rock music magazine and, um, every issue we do an interview with a mainstream band, and we print the entire interview word-for-word, um, you know, cuz we don't want, we don't want to try to make you out to be anything you're not, you know? Whether it's more spiritual or less and … We commit ourselves to printing word-for-word everything that is said in the conversation—the ahs, the ums, the wells, the hmmms … everything and …

TVL: "I guess I said a lot in my interview then." (laughs)

Well, you know, cuz we're interested in … in what you have to say on, you know, the topics that, you know, we happen to bring up, and everything and, uh, we know that spirituality usually makes an imprint on an artist's work in one way or …

TVL: "Let me add to that then. I will say that spirituality is definitely a part of my life. I guess music would be my religion. That's where I've found, what I would call salvation, you know? Self-expression and, you know, making music … it's just the only thing that I really keep coming back to, and it makes me feel exalted. So, I just like the idea of having spirituality and, you know, expressing it. So, I'll close with that."

It was great talking to you.

TVL: "Alright, you too."

And I wish you complete success with everything that A Perfect Circle's going to be doing and whatever you may do as a solo project.

TVL: "Thank you."

Yeah, any chance of a solo project?

TVL: "I have a band that I'm working on as we speak. My music is called Enemy. It's another rock band. And, uh, hopefully, when we're done with this, I can get out with that and, you know, while Maynard's doing Tool, and everyone sort of gets back to their so-called life ... (To person in the background) 'Okay, I think we're done, James.' ('Oh, cool,' James says in the background). See you, Gordon."

[Originally printed in September/October '00 Issue #85]

"People tend to assume that, because you have 'become a Christian,' that you have become like them."

—Jeremy Enigk

SUNNY DAY REAL ESTATE

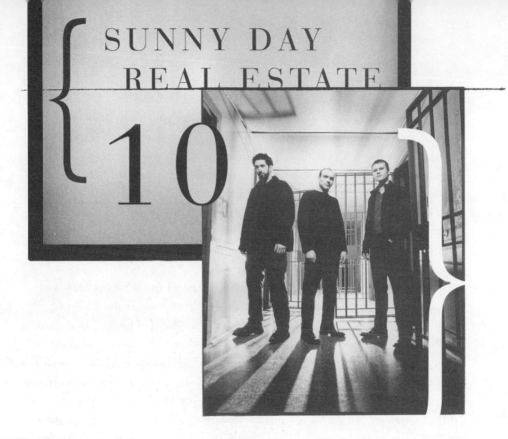

10

[Feature Article by David M. Pogge]

Though only in existence in the public consciousness a year before their initial breakup, the Seattle quartet known as Sunny Day Real Estate did more to shape the musical landscape of their time than the vast majority of flannel clad radio clones of the early '90s could ever have come close to achieving. While grunge was taking the airwaves by storm and Kurt Cobain was reaching the level of a pop culture deity, Sunny Day Real Estate lay comfortably in the shadows, crafting an album that would define a genre and generate hordes of adherents and imitators. *Diary*, while only scratching the surface of mainstream exposure, was a pivotal release of beauty and aggression that perfectly enveloped the soul-searching angst that Eddie

Vedder had been trying so hard to effectively communicate. Emo as a genre had long since been established, but never had it been so poignantly defined.

Unfortunately, nearly as quickly as they had appeared, they were gone, leaving us only with an obscure posthumous collection of songs clothed in a solid pink cover as a parting gift. Rumors spread like a virus as to what caused their demise. Through all of the muddling of fact and fiction, the prevailing belief was that vocalist Jeremy Enigk's newfound faith in Christ had caused the split. Furthering this notion was Jeremy's bold and eloquently written profession of faith posted on the band's web board. As with most rumors, this commonly accepted explanation was only half true.

"It was ultimately the catalyst," Jeremy clarifies, "I think Sunny Day was going to break up anyway. It was inevitable; we all were really kind of confused and young and not really sure what we wanted to do." In the midst of this naive confusion, Jeremy was able to find strength in the assurance of God's love and salvation. "I wouldn't have found that strength anywhere else ... when you have someone like God on your side ... you don't need anything. You don't need music or money ... you know, you don't need any of these things anymore. All you want and all you need is love, so I had no problem quitting the band, because it didn't hold anything of value to me anymore."

Following the breakup, Jeremy went on to pursue a solo career, guitarist Dan Hoerner started a tree farm in Washington, and bassist Nate Mendel and drummer Will Goldsmith went on to join the Foo Fighters. All the while, Sunny Day's popularity only grew and expanded, until a reunion was all but mandatory. In the fall of '98, Sunny Day Real Estate returned minus Nate with the critically acclaimed *How It Feels To Be Something On*, and silenced even the most jaded critic with the album's strikingly unique Beatle-esque melodies and Jeremy's distinct crooning vocals. Two years and several tours later, Sunny Day have once again re-emerged and redefined themselves with *The Rising Tide*, perhaps the band's most remarkable work to date; the quintessential collection reveals more common ground with the likes of Rush and Genesis than protegés such as Mineral.

"I think every step of the way on this latest album, we all gave 110 percent," says Jeremy. "We were all there to do whatever we needed to do to make it better. Although we didn't have all the time we could have used or that we needed, we definitely took more time to think about things and to really experiment and not just throw out our guitar lines and our drum parts and call it good." In the end, though, they had every reason to call it good. Pleasantly grandiose melodies that surpass perfection and superb production shine through without dispute. However, the beautiful lyrics that convey the universal themes of unconditional love and the desire for change may even surpass the quality of the music.

"There wasn't really initially one theme that we ever tried to put out," Jeremy explains of the album's lyrical concept, "but ultimately, the one theme that I kind of get out of the album is ... you know, the title itself, kind of a *Rising Tide* ... is, is kind of the rising of all the chaos ... our earth is just slowly kind of dying, you know, and our world, and the way that we treat everybody, is just wrong and is just ugly. And, ultimately the *Rising Tide*, you know, for me ... exposes those things as much as it can creatively, you know? Yet, [it] leaves it open for hope and change. That's what I get out of the rising tide, is that it's really, like, in the midst of all of the chaos and all of the garbage and the (expletive), there is beauty, you know, and that we do have the power to basically, do what we need to do, to change our world, to change our perspectives."

Since the reunion, it has generally been taken for granted that Jeremy has retained his faith in Christ as a foundation for his life and art. Even major publications like *Guitar World* and *Alternative Press*, not to mention the majority of his fans, label him a "born again." Apparently, no one has bothered to ask Jeremy. When asked if God was still an important part of his life, Jeremy replied with admirable honesty in the midst of uncertainty.

"Yeah, I mean, heavily, but I'm not speaking in, like, a religious way, or, like, going to church ... I'm not even talking about accepting Jesus Christ as your Savior and all that lingo that Christians have kind of created. You know, the whole personal Savior thing ... that's not really what I mean. But as much as God is a part of everybody's life every day, you know, I think God is a part of my life."

Naturally, with the popular assumption being that Jeremy is still a practicing

Christian, the issue of his faith comes up regularly in conversations with fans. "It gets annoying," Jeremy admits. "It gets really annoying, because people tend to assume that, because you have 'become a Christian,' that you have become like them, or become what they think a Christian is. It's been tough at times, because I can't talk about God, and I can't have a deep theological discussion every day. And I can't think God is rad every day, or even believe in God every day. And when I'm on tour and I'm constantly having people want to talk about that and know how I feel about God, it's too much, you know? I just can't go there... It's painful and it's difficult. And so I get slightly annoyed, but I don't blame the people, because it was something that I wanted to happen, and that's one of the reasons that I wrote that crazy letter."

[Originally printed in November/December '00 Issue #86]

"You don't have
to go to church
to believe
in God."

—Chad Kroeger

photo by Daniel Moss

In case you haven't noticed, Roadrunner Records isn't a "Death Metal Only" label. They've recently added some very promising alt-rock bands to their roster, like Johnny Q. Public, Podunk, Nickelback, and others. When we heard Nickelback's The State album, with its radio-friendly hit "Leader Of Men," we knew we should talk to them. Listen in as editor Doug Van Pelt talks with vocalist/guitarist Chad Kroeger.

Hold on just a second and let me grab my questions. Okay, I've got a tape recorder rolling, so we'll fire away. Uh, well first I have to say, I love your songs.

CK: "Right on."

I'm really enjoying this new album.

CK: "Thank you very much."

Speaking of *The State*, what exactly did you do to it for the U.S. re-release?

CK: "Um, just changed the artwork, that's it."

Okay, well for an indie release, you had some great production.

CK: "Cool."

Yeah, so what is on the agenda, as far as the summer goes and touring plans?

CK: "Well, we're just finishing up with Creed right now, and then we're gonna do some more shows with Three Doors Down. We did a large tour with them already. Then I think we are gonna go out and headline some stuff, and UPO is going to come with us."

How is it touring with Creed?

CK: "Awesome!"

Cool.

CK: "We played in front of, you know, 10,000 people every night."

Wow. That's great. What part of Canada are you from?

CK: "Vancouver."

All right. What was your ... what kind of impact did the whole Seattle grunge explosion have on you, musically, and just your social life, if any?

CK: "Um. Uh, probably just the same as it did on everybody else. I mean, there was a lot of good music coming out of Seattle at the same time, and, you know, everybody was diggin' it."

Cool. What was the brief history of your band prior to recording *The State*, and how did you get the momentum that this album kind of gave you?

CK: "Well, we started off with $4,000, and we went to Vancouver and recorded seven songs. A couple of managers heard it and put it on the radio for us, and then we just started to build a following, and, uh ... then we fired them, actually ... when we were recording *The State*. We just sort of realized their limitations and thought we could do a better job of ... you know, the whole thing ourselves, and I handled all the radio promotion in Canada and got the song as high as nineteen on the rock charts, and we sold 10,000 copies on our own. And that's when the record companies started trickling in."

Cool. How did you end up picking Roadrunner? I know that they're, you know—predominantly they have been the U.S. kings of death metal, and now they have released about a half a dozen really good, uh, modern rock albums.

CK: "They're changing, you know. They don't want to be that anymore. You know, they wanna branch out and do all kinds of radio stuff—stuff that's a little bit more accessible than Slipknot and Cold Chamber and Fear Factory and all that stuff that, you know, usually isn't gonna get on the radio unless they do a cover of something else."

Right.

CK: "And they hired a really great radio team—stole most of them from RCA New York, brought them over. They were really excited about the record, and they promised us a top ten record in six months. Now they've given it to us."

Wow! That's good for them and you.

CK: "Yeah."

That's cool. Well, what do you think of Jesus Christ?

CK: "What do I think of Jesus Christ? Um, great guy ... good golf game. (laughs) I don't know. Can you narrow that down?"

Okay, what do you think of His claims to be the Way, the Truth, and the Life—"no one comes to the Father but by Me?"

CK: "Oh, (long pause) um, (long pause again, and a big sigh) Ya know what? I'm gonna keep my philosophical beliefs to myself on this one (laugh). Um, I believe in Jesus Christ, but I also believe in a lot of different things, um ... and, uh, I don't know. I'm more like—if you're a good person and you got a good soul, uh, there is life beyond earth, and I don't think they just have to go through Jesus Christ. Um ... that would make a lot of Asians extremely upset."

Uh-huh. Have you heard that there's like millions and millions of Christians in Asia, and specifically China—the home church movement has exploded.

CK: "Oh well, that's fine. (laughs) Okay, well then how about then, uh, there's gonna be a lot of upset East Indians. How's that?"

Yeah. There you go. Um ... well, do you think that claim was, uh, you know, an accurate one that He made? Or do you think that someone else gave it to Him? Or do you think that He was just out to lunch by saying that He's the only way?

CK: "I don't know. I didn't know Him personally, and I didn't hear Him say the quote so, you know, uh, it's hard for me to judge."

Uh-huh.

CK: "Um ... yeah, I don't know ... These are, like, heavy, heavy questions that I hate using my position in a band for political or religious platforms. I can't stand people that preach. The only thing that I preach is, you know,

'Hey ... smoke pot!' (laughs) That's it. Um, and I think that people that use those and that abuse their position in bands for political or religious platforms ... uh, I don't know. It's supposed to be about the music. Ya know? Although, in terms of Rage Against the Machine ... um, I've got to give those guys some credit. They sort of do it the right way, you know. They sort of preach in their music, but it's not even so much preaching; it's just like, 'Open your eyes and look around at what's going on.' It's that sort of thing."

Uh-huh.

CK: "It's not preaching so much. It's just providing you with a sarcastic spoonful of information. And I'm not one to, uh, you know, Nickelback is not a Christian band. Nickelback is not a political band, and it never will be with four guys that write, you know, rock songs? If you dig 'em, you dig 'em. And if you don't, you don't."

Did you write the song "Not Leaving Yet?"

CK: "Yeah."

Did you have a grandfather that had some influence on your life or ...

CK: "That song's actually about my grandmother, and I'm saying the first lines through her. 'Come lie next to me, Jesus Christ' ... on her death bed."

Uh-huh. Isn't there a line in there about not using grandfather as bait?

CK: "Yeah, my grandfather passed away, and it was sort of like, 'Don't use my ...' It's sort of like me saying to Jesus Christ, 'Don't take my grandmother yet, and don't use my grandfather as bait.'"

Gotcha. What sort of other influences ... Well, what influences do you draw from when you are writing a song? How do you put the ideas on paper?

CK: "Uh, I actually come up with the riffs first. I come up with the music first, and then I start humming a melody over it, and the song just starts to take shape. I'll spit out a few sentences and a few phrases here and there.

Then it just all starts to take shape, and then I sort of realize what the song's gonna be, you know? What the subject matter is, and I just (take it) from there. That's typically how it goes."

Uh-huh. How long have you been writing songs, and how long have you been making music?

CK: "Well, I've been playing the guitar for twelve years, and I've been singing for four. So I mean, ever since I've picked up a guitar, I've been writing my own, you know, little riffs here and little riffs there. I don't know ... I think I've only really seriously been writing songs for about five years, and I've been in Nickelback for four."

Was the choice of using G. Garth, or "GGG ... Garth Richardson," having anything to do with the Rage Against the Machine guys?

CK: "No. He lives in Vancouver, so that made it very easy, very accessible. It didn't hurt that, you know, he comes with a great résumé—including Rage Against the Machine."

Yeah, he sure does.

CK: "He stutters, that's why it actually reads, 'GGG ... Garth.'"

(laughs) Is that serious?

CK: "Yeah. Absolutely. He's got a horrible stutter, and, uh, that's how it actually says in his contract: 'Mr. Richardson's name will appear as GGG ... Garth on all records, on all advertisements for the record over half a page,' you know? 'Yada, yada, yada ...' It all has to read: 'Mixed by GGG ... Garth.'"

Huh. You'd think that somebody who stuttered would be self-conscious about it—and having your nickname ...

CK: "I think Rage probably started it, and since they did, he'd kind of liked to keep it going."

Uh-huh. That's very interesting. Well, considering your opinion on using a band for an agenda, what's your opinion about Creed? A lot of people consider them to be pushing an agenda or ... a lot of their songs are about spiritual things, and God is a frequent topic.

CK: "I don't think they're pushing it. I just think they might be topics that they are using. I definitely don't hear him in between songs going, 'You know, you need to devote your life to Jesus Christ, and if you don't, you're going to burn in hell ...' You know? I think we definitely don't hear that from them."

Um hum. What do you think about the prospect of a hell and a heaven? You mentioned kind of an afterlife or something. What are your thoughts on how that breaks down, and what are the details?

CK: "Um, my visions of heaven and hell are sort of mine, and I think that I'm going to keep them mine. I don't think that it's anybody else's business, really—the way I view those things— and I don't think that anyone's going to be interested in my vision of heaven and hell, anyway. I just like to, you know ... I'm into the beat—the groove and melody. If I can get my song stuck in somebody's head, then I'm doing my job."

Uh-huh.

CK: "You know ... if I can get your foot tappin' and your head bobbin,' then I'm doing my job."

I think you're doing a good job, but, uh ... So, are you telling me that, if you're reading a magazine and Zach De LaRocha or somebody—or Bono— is talkin' about how he thinks about God, that you're just gonna close the magazine shut and throw it down and say, "That ticks me off. I don't want to read about this!?" Or would you actually find it interesting?

CK: "Um, if he chose to talk about it then, you know, I might read it. I don't really care what ... I might want to wait till I get to the next part of information that I do find interesting. Um, I don't really care how anybody else views heaven or hell. I obviously just care about the way I view it."

We, uh, have been publishing *HM* for fifteen years now, and we've been doing a column called "What So and So Says." You fill in the name of band in the blank. You know, "What Nickelback Says." And our magazine covers the Christian hard music genre, but with every issue we depart from that, and we interview somebody from Metallica or Morbid Angel or Megadeth or Extreme or King Diamond or Creed or whoever, and uh, we found it very interesting ... They're popular. A lot of people do like to hear what someone has to say about this topic. In fact, we're hoping to get a book published and publish, like, all eighty-plus interviews we've done on this subject. Some people like to ... It's just intriguing, it's not your run-of-the-mill, "So, tell me about your guitar setup? So, tell me about this new tour? So, tell me about your video? What does this song mean?"

CK: "Yeah. I mean, of course, that sure gets boring. But there's ... I don't know. I just, uh—I honestly hate discussing my beliefs with other people, because they are mine. Ya, know? If you and I wanted to have a discussion, we could have one, but I definitely don't—I'm really not interested in having the rest of the world know what I think, or what my beliefs are, because they're mine, and they're more precious to me than the music or anything else—and that's why ... I don't know, I don't know. That's exposing a little more of me than I am willing to do."

Alright. What are your goals in your music? Do you, uh ... If you start spilling some of that out in a lyric and (it) just kind of flows out, are you gonna kind of stop yourself and say, "Hey, I don't want to go there ..." or "I'll just keep that song to myself," or would you be willing to, kind of, express these thoughts in song?

CK: "I actually express them all the time, and it's uh, metaphoric."

Uh-huh.

CK: "It's sort of like a little riddle. If you figure it out, then you get a ... You know, then you figure it out, and you get to know what I'm referring to. And, if you don't, then you don't, and that's part of the puzzle."

Gotcha. What are your thoughts on the legalization of weed?

CK: "Um, I don't really know. I don't know that they should legalize it. Well, I don't know. There's so many points—good and bad. You know, some of the good points are that: You've never really heard of anybody getting in a vehicle stoned and killing people. People don't even really like to drive when they're stoned. You don't really hear somebody hitting a bong and then beating up their wife or getting rowdy. That doesn't happen. But it happens all the time with booze. You know, people drive drunk; they kill people. People drink in bars, and they drink at home, and they get violent. Alcohol definitely provides a little bit of a violent outlet to people that are, you know, so inclined. And I just don't think that weed does that. It doesn't do it for me ... And then I think a lot of the romance of pot would be lost if it was legalized."

Uh-huh.

CK: "But I do think that they should definitely lighten up. You could carry, like, twenty-one grams in Vancouver, and if you get caught with it, they just take it away. And we've got coffee shops where you can smoke it, and it's up to you if you want to smoke it, but if a cop walks in, they'll just take it away, you know, unless you're carrying a lot. And even if you're carrying a lot, all they do is give you a ticket. They don't even give you a court date!"

Uh-huh.

CK: "You've got to be growing more than, like, fifty plants—I think it is—before you get charged with harvesting. If it's, like, forty-nine plants, then it's a slap on the wrist. So, it's very, very tame, and I like that. I think a lot of people like that. I mean, that's the whole thing with Amsterdam. That's all they talk about. It's like: hash bars and, 'Oh, you can do this, and you can smoke legally, and you can do this, and you can do this,' and it's like, 'Well, we've been doing this in Vancouver for years.'"

Uh-huh. It sure is a big difference from that, and a policeman going by a garage and smelling something, and a seventeen-year-old or eighteen-year-old gets thrown in prison with, you know, murderers and thugs.

CK: "That's a little silly. When we were in Nevada, there were some kids (who) were telling me that somebody actually did get caught with one marijuana seed. They did six months. That is ridiculous. You know, I mean, that guy, he wasn't trying to hurt anybody. It's such a small crime. It's sort of like drinking during prohibition. You know, to look back on that now, we think that's silly. You know, that was ridiculous. (And) people are getting ... That's something that I just don't have a tolerance for."

Uh-huh.

CK: "That Nazi (expletive) is just a little crazy."

Have you ever thought about, uh, you know, having children and telling your kids, "Hey, as far as your religion or your faith, I'm going to let you decide when you get older?" Or do ...

CK: "That is exactly what I'm going to do. You know, it's like, 'This is what will happen if you do this, and this is what will happen if you do this.' You know, 'Just do it wisely.' I would honestly rather have my kids smoke dope than drink. If I had to choose one or the other, I would definitely take pot. You know, 'cause they're not gonna get into vehicles and kill anybody or themselves, you know? I'll just provide them with the facts and let them make their own decisions and hope that they're going to do it responsibly— the same way I did."

Uh-huh. What about with faith and religion?

CK: "I don't know. After I have children, I might want to go to church a little more than I do now. That's another one of my beliefs. Um, you don't have to go to church to believe in God."

Uh-huh.

CK: "You don't have to ... I mean, that's part of that whole ... Have you seen the movie *Stigmata*?"

Yeah.

CK: "They had a couple topics ... I mean, most of the flick was (expletive), but they had a couple of topics in there that were really interesting. You know, the fact that, uh, Christ never said that anybody ever had to go to a church to worship. It's like, uh, I think the pope has got mafia-esque power that he shouldn't have. You know? I'm not necessarily ... I'm ... (laughs) Now I'm going to start a controversy. I've got other people walking through the bus going, 'Wait a minute! The pope's what!?!' (laughs)

"I just think that, you know, if you believe in what you believe in, you know, you don't have to go to a church, and you don't have to send money to some evangelist. The things that you do in your life ... I don't know ... It just ... it's all like, ugh! I really don't want to get into it. I'm, like, trying to avoid this. I'm trying to like, stay on the rocks. By jumping into the water, it's going to be a lo-o-o-o-n-n-g conversation."

Uh-huh. (laughs)

CK: "Anyhow, I guess I'll cross that bridge when I get to it—as far as the children go."

Uh-huh. I think it's kind of a revolutionary statement—what we heard in that movie about how you don't have to be in a sanctuary to be in a sanctuary ... quote-unquote. I think that's so true ... and some people really need to hear that.

CK: "Yeah. Why don't they let us see the rest of the Dead Sea scrolls?"

Uh-huh.

CK: "'Cause I think that they say the exact same thing, you know? And the Church doesn't want us to see that ... 'cause their whole—everything that they are would fall apart."

Uh-huh.

CK: "And, you know, uh, even if the Bible is just a story, isn't it a good set of guidelines to live by?"

Uh-huh.

CK: "You know, if you have to use the fact to scare somebody, saying, 'You know, if you don't abide by these rules and you don't treat everybody the way that you would like to be treated, and try and live a good and decent life, that you'll go to some place that is unimaginably horrible—with fire and brimstone and the whole nine yards ...' It's like, I'm so ... I'm such a fifty-fifty guy. I'm such a, you know, half a scientist and half a believer." (long pause)

Is somebody saying something to you?

CK: "No, I was just waiting for you."

Okay, I thought that you were in the middle of a sentence.

CK: "No, no, they're chattin' back there in the room."

Okay. Yeah. I think that, uh, some people, you know ... Not all churches, of course, preach fire and brimstone. I think that, uh ... Well, I go to church because I know that, uh, it ... it provides kind of a health factor for me. I'm encouraged and I'm around people that, uh, build me up. And ... if I go through some tough times, I have people there that can help me; whereas, if I was off on my own and never attended church, I would be likely to, you know, set myself up to become arrogant or, you know, come up with some looney toon ideas ...

CK: "Do you think that, uh, if you don't go to church that you're gonna become arrogant?"

Uh ... Well, let's put it this way: A lot of Christians I know, if they decide they're gonna stop going to church ... a couple years down the road, usually all of them need it somehow. Or they, they find themselves out in left field where their life gets shipwrecked somehow.

CK: (big, huge laugh) "Ha ha ha ha ha. Wow!"

Maybe there's another way to put that ... I go to church ...

CK: "So, that's like a ... that's like a fear, that, 'Gee, if I don't go, if I don't go to church, um, my life is going to get steered in the wrong direction and I'm no longer going to be a good person, and I'm going to be lost. I'll be lost if I don't go to church.' I just think that's so, that's so silly."

Yeah, but I didn't say that. I just ... I don't have a fear about not going to church.

CK: "I didn't say you ... (laughs) but I think that a lot of people do feel that way."

Uh-huh. Or some people, maybe, present the Church or present themselves or their organization as a, 'If you leave us, you're history.' And, of course, that's just controlling by fear and manipulating (But) If you're truly encouraging people and saying ...

CK: "I prefer to call that brainwashing."

Yeah.

CK: "(And) that scares me more than, you know ... I mean, you might as well call your pastor or your priest or your minister ... uh, you might as well be under Charles Manson."

A cult leader ...

CK: "Yeah, or any kind of cult leader."

Yeah.

CK: "I mean, that's one thing that really turns me off about religion—about organized religion."

Uh-huh. But: What turned the early Christians on to church? I mean, why did they go from house to house and break bread and pray? I mean, what is it about those things that turn people on, and if those things are healthy, would it not be healthy to go to church?

CK: "Those things are healthy, but not always ... uh, not all people involved in the Church are healthy."

Right ... and, of course, nobody's completely healthy.

CK: "Yeah, that's why you have, you know, priests molesting choir boys and all the things that go wrong with churches."

Uh-huh.

CK: "Because ... I mean, that's just one more thing that just, you know, it's the red stain on the whole white curtain. It's just a ..."

Yeah. I guess the whole reason I bring it up is ... I run into this so much where, you know: "You don't need church! Church is bogus!" And one part of me says, "Well, no." I mean, the church I go to is not bogus. You know ... our pastor doesn't stand up and try to choke anybody with what he says. It's a healthy thing, and I don't hear enough people, you know, telling anybody else what is good about church. You know, it's true. You don't have to, you don't have to go to a church to find God, and the Bible makes that definitely clear. (But) uh ... all the churches aren't corrupt.

CK: "No. That's absolutely true, and those are the good ones. Um, it's the other guys that ruin it for some of the other people that are, you know, just on the fence. They sort of, uh, tarnish the image."

Uh-huh.

CK: "You know, to the point where it makes anybody who's on the fence not want to go to church and not want to belong to one."

Uh-huh.

CK: "But I've, I've really gotta bolt. They're ... they're, uh, everyone's screamin' at me here. We've gotta go do a photo session. Have you got enough stuff to work with?"

Yeah. I think so. I hope I get to see you guys. If you're ever in Austin, Texas, I'd love to chat some more, maybe we can have that talk.

CK: "Absolutely. Absolutely."

[Originally printed in January/February '01 Issue #87]

"I wouldn't
call myself a
religious person,
but I wouldn't
call myself,
like, an atheist
or anything,
you know?"

—Ryan Pope

THE
GET UP KIDS

To the delight and dismay of many, Kansas City's The Get Up Kids have taken their pop-laced Midwestern angst ("emo") well beyond community halls and scenester clubs. With the support of Vagrant Records, and through their own Vagrant imprint, Heroes and Villains, The Kids have sold more than 70,000 copies of their album Something to Write Home About, and at the time of the interview were playing between Weezer and Ozma on the nationally sold-out Yahoo! Outloud Tour, a spot they won via online voting at Yahoo.com. After we checked out the opening night of the tour here in Austin, Managing Editor Jason E. Dodd called drummer Ryan Pope for a brief interview ...

Tell me about the Weezer/Yahoo! Out Loud Tour.

RP: "It's going good. We have only been on it for about a week now, and we have another three weeks left. All of the shows have been sold out, you know. Uh, I don't know, it's been fun."

What are your thoughts on Weezer and Ozma, playing with them so far?

RP: "Um, It's been fun. They're good bands." (long pause ... laugh)

How do feel about the overt corporate sponsorship of the tour?

RP: "Um, I'm not opposed to it. I think that ... some degrees of corporate sponsorship can get ridiculous, and uh ... this particular one, I don't think it's ... I think it's done well. Let me put it that way. The tickets for the shows were really low, you know; the people seemed to be, like, pretty laid back about it. So, I don't know. It made it possible to ... I don't know. I guess have so many people ... I guess it got Weezer out on a tour."

Yeah, that's a cool thing. I know that this has been out for, like, a year now, but tell me about *Something to Write Home About*.

RP: "Uh, yeah. I guess we made it ... we made that record about a year and a half ago. I don't know, it's our second full record, and ... well, third if you count, like, EPs and whatnot ... and I think it's our best record up to date."

Do you guys have plans for a new album yet?

RP: "Yeah, we are actually working on it right now, writing and stuff."

Any kind of projected release date?

RP: "It will come out probably in January 2002."

And that's with Vagrant Records, also?

RP: "Yep, it's with Vagrant and Heroes and Villains."

Which is your imprint.

RP: "Yep."

And you guys actually manage that imprint?

RP: "Um, you know, in a round-about way, yeah. We work together with Vagrant, kind of like, you know, as a partnership."

Reading through your press kit and other stuff that I've seen in other zines and whatnot, and, you know, also from talking to kids, there seems to be a dichotomous respect/backlash in the underground and mainstream for The Get Up Kids, as well as for bands like Jimmy Eat World, Juliana Theory, At the Drive In, etc. Have you perceived that at all?

RP: "Yeah, I would say so. A lot of people, um, they want your band to always be like, 'their band,' you know? They want to basically keep you in their pocket and not share you with anyone. Kind of that whole mentality of, 'Well, I knew about them first,' or, 'You're not cool enough to like this band,' or whatever. So, I don't know ... I think we have, you know, gotten away from that corner. We don't really have to deal with that anymore, but there was a point when we were dealing with a lot of kids saying, like, 'You guys are selling out,' or, 'I don't like going to your concerts anymore, because there are too many people there,' or, you know, stuff like that. We're just like, 'ppshh ... whatever,' you know? We really don't care."

I read in *The Big Takeover* ... I don't remember who wrote it, but in their review of your album, they said something like, "So, mainstream America is finally noticing these bands," referring to The Get Up Kids and I guess your, uh, compatriots, "is it going to be Nirvana all over again?" That seems like a silly question, but it's kind of interesting at the same time. Do you think that there is going to be a resurgence of "underground rock" into the mainstream, and do you think that you guys are kind of spearheading that?

RP: "I think that it's kind of already happening, but it's happening much slower and more natural, you know? Like, I think a lot of people maybe are sick of the mainstream music, and sick of being like ... sick of the radio and being, like, spoon fed, and they are tired of *NSYNC and stuff like that, you know? And they ... um ... especially for everyone who buys, say, an *NSYNC or Backstreet Boys record, there is going to be someone else who is going to be like ... there is going to be a backlash, you know? It's just natural. So, I think that ... I'm not going to say that everything is becoming ..."

What was that? Your phone cut off.

RP: "I just think that ... I think people are searching more for good music. Napster and stuff like that has helped, because it's made everything more accessible for music."

Why do you think that so many of your generation are connecting with your songs?

RP: "Maybe because ... geez, that's a hard question. Maybe because we're ... I think most of our songs are kind of about [stuff that] a lot of people can relate to maybe, in their own weird way, whatever that means. You know, they're about, like, everyday life, or normal things that everyone usually experiences. Other than that, it's hard to say, but uh, it's definitely a good thing."

Tell me about touring with MxPx.

RP: "Well, that was about two and a half years ago."

Was it that long ago?

RP: "It was about two years ago, yeah. Um, it was kind of a newer thing for our band. That was our first, basically, big opening tour that we ever did, you know what I mean? It was cool. We gained a lot of fans. It was odd to play in front of the, like, the 'Christian' market, you know?"

Did it bother you that they are Christians?

RP: "Not at all. I think it's a good thing. It didn't bother us at all ... You mean as the band or the fans?"

Well, both I guess.

RP: "No, not at all. The band didn't bother us. We're friends with those guys still. As far as the fans, um, no, that's fine with us. We don't try to like mold ... um ... pick our fans and, you know, say they have to be a certain way. That's stupid, you know?"

Yeah, that's cool. What do you think of Jesus?

RP: "What do I think of Jesus? (laughs) Um, you know, I don't know. I have mixed feelings about religion. So, I wouldn't call myself a religious person, but I wouldn't call myself, like, an atheist or anything, you know?"

Yeah.

RP: "I ... um ... I don't know ... uh ... Next question!"

Alright ... tell me about Reggie and the Full Effect.

RP: "It's a side project that our keyboard player does, James Dewees. It's basically kind of a ... he's a really funny guy, and it's kind of his thing that he's been doing for a really long time. I guess it started when we all lived together. Like, me and my brother Rob and James and he would write these really funny, crazy pop songs, or whatever, and then we were like, 'Hey, put that stuff out,' so he did."

What are you currently listening to?

RP: "Um, I'm listening to Bob Dylan ... um ... The Replacements, and have you heard this band called The Doves? They are from England. I've just pretty recently kind of gotten into that CD, and I've been listening to *Rubber Soul* a lot, the Beatles record. It's a record that you never get tired of."

Where are The Get Up Kids going from here? What are your plans?

RP: "Our plan for now is to go make a really good record. And to enjoy what we are doing, have fun, and keep touring ... nothing too uncommon. I guess, become a better band, you know."

Are you approaching your songwriting a little differently for this next album, like, do you think that you've learned anything in the last year or so that you think is going to affect your songwriting?

RP: "Oh, yeah, definitely. We've come a long way, as far as understanding songs and stuff like that, you know."

What are some things that you've learned about songwriting?

RP: "Um, basically, we all started playing in bands since we were fifteen years old, and now we're all in our twenties, or whatever, and we are a bit more ... I want to say more educated, as far as music goes, we hope at least. And, uh, I think our taste has become more obvious, maybe."

What do you mean?

RP: "Like, what we are into. As a band, we kind of learned how to focus that better than before, and as a band you learn how to play what you want to, and, I don't know, focus better."

[Originally printed in May/June '01 Issue #89]

"If it works
for you,
if it gets
you through
the night,
great."

—Henry Rollins

13

HENRY ROLLINS

I didn't expect this Henry Rollins interview to be a big deal. My coworkers were nervous, though, 'cause they'd heard reports about how difficult an interview with Henry could be. I'd been doing this for over a decade, so I approached it as just another challenge. The inner-office pacing and nervousness started to bug me, making me wonder how this would turn out. Dealing with a "difficult interview subject" is just one of a journalist's challenges, and, if you've crossed that barrier enough times, you figure out how to get through it. I have to admit, though, when he called me a "prick," it was easy to envision those veins in his neck bulging, and that glaring mean look he's famous for. It never felt like the interview got back on track, but re-reading it later relieves me, as I see more than three-word responses coming from him. The rest of the day, however, was odd. That feeling of

having your nerves rattled, like the "fight or flight syndrome," doesn't go
away quickly. This was countered by the excitement of friends as I relayed
the story to them. Really, though, it was no big deal. Yeah, sure, pal!

Some artists are fortunate enough to make their living doing music, and
doing well enough to call their own shots, etc. Some artists can keep themselves busy by doing a number of things, like acting, TV, movie work,
production, writing, etc., to where they can take a year off if they want to.
Other artists are successful enough to where, sales-wise, to where they can
keep their record deal, but not selling enough to where they can break out of
the cycle of having to release a new album every year and a half or so, and
then tour to support it. Where are you in your career, and how do you feel
about where you're at?

HR: "I do what I want, when I want, and I feel really good about it."

That's a great place to be. How is the publishing company going?

HR: "Fine."

Good. On the recent research interview book, you said you've had some
major struggles with the book industry.

HR: "Well, it's ... it's hard to get people to read. And when you're independent ... ahh ... [a] book company, you're running in direct competition with
huge book companies who can buy a lot more promotional space at Barnes
& Noble , and Borders ... which are ... unfortunately the two main places
where people now get their books."

Uh-huh. Yep, I understand that's like a microcosm or almost a direct parallel
to the record industry in a lot of ways.

HR: "Well, the record industry there's a lot more ... ways to move around in
it."

Uh-huh.

HR: "More avenues open to you, but not so much with the book thing."

Gotcha. Do you find that you have a separate audience for your writing spoken-word and your musical recordings and performances?

HR: "Umm ... Yeah ... I think ... you probably see some older types at the talking shows that you might not see at the band shows."

Hmm ... Why do you think that is?

HR: "A lot of people my age would probably listen to *The Best of Sting* or something."

If you were going to, what do you think you'd retire from first—music or spoken word?

HR: "Probably the music. Probably the music would beat me out of it "

(laughs) What are your feelings on the "new" punk rock? How much in common do you think Blink 182 has with Black Flag?

HR: "Ahh ... I don't ... I can't say I've ever heard a Blink 182 song all the way through. I saw a video for that 'Rock Show' video ... I thought it was really fun ... really funny. It was really cool. Umm ... but I thought they were more like a pop band from what it sounded like to me, than you know any kind of big attitude, or you know, hard-hitting music. It just seemed kind of like, very Decedents sounding pop band."

Uh-huh.

HR: "But, ya know, that's the only song I've ever heard of theirs so I can't ... I can't really give you a critique."

What about just in general, some of the new punk rock that's on the radio and what not?

HR: "Well, quite honestly, I've never heard a Slipknot song ... ever. I've never heard a Limp Bizkit song all the way through. I've never heard a Rage Against the Machine song all the way through. I really am pretty unaware of a lot of what's going on out there. I've never heard a Korn song all the way through."

Uh-huh. Kinda like you've heard bits and pieces of them though ...

HR: "Well you run into it on the radio and on video."

Yeah.

HR: "Umm ... but I've never really sat down and checked it out."

A lot of music historians and whatnot, they ahh ... They give a lot of credence to British punk rock music. Do you think a lot of this credence is deserved, and if so, why or why not?

HR: "Oh ahh .. I think ahh ... some of the best music in the last thirty years, forty years has come out of the U.K."

Uh-huh.

HR: "And a lot of great punk rock stuff has come out of there. A lot of that music I listen to very much to this day."

In your opinion, what are some of the current hot spots or cities around the world that you love traveling to, and are any of these making important punk rock?

HR: "Well ... like I said to you three times now, I'm not really up on the world of punk rock."

Uh-huh.

HR: "As far as great cities to play in, I play in about one hundred a year, and so ... ya know ... I don't know, pick a country. There's always great cities."

What about just important rock 'n' roll? Do you feel that there's some important rock 'n' roll being made, and if so where at?

HR: "I don't know if there's any particular city ... um ... there's great music scenes. Like Chicago has always had a very strong local music scene where there's a lot of interesting music happening. Um ... Washington D.C, New York, ahh ... Los Angeles, San Francisco. Those are places where there's always something interesting happening."

Uh-huh. If Henry Rollins had twenty-four hours left to live, what would be some of the top priorities on your to-do list, and why?

HR: "Ahh ... I'd probably be ahh ... giving away ahh ... all my stuff and kinda make my things. The record collection and all that stuff go to like good homes, and ahh ... definitely deleting my hard drive."

Do you think you'll ever marry?

HR: "No."

Why not?

HR: "'Cause I don't want to be tied down to anybody."

How did you get roped into hosting that current horror TV show *Night Visions*?

HR: "How did I get roped into it?!?"

Yeah.

HR: "Why do you characterize it like that? Are you just characterizing it like that, or are you trying to be a flippant little prick?"

More of the flippant side.

HR: "Oh, well, don't get flippant with me unless you want to get in my face and do it, and then we'll see how flippant you are. On the phone it's a little bit too much of the ahh ... the casual observer shooting the wounded after the war is over."

Yeah, I didn't mean to do that.

HR: "Yeah, you don't want to do that with me."

I think you came pretty close to a Rod Serling, which is a compliment. Are you a *Twilight Zone* guy?

HR: "Yeah."

Well, let's just move on. What initially gave you the confidence to do spoken word performances?

HR: "I have a desire to communicate. And it's fun to go up there and tell stories and have a point of view, and have an opinion, and have it received ... and I ahh ... think it's pretty cool in this day and age when you got a lot of high velocity, high tech entertainment or just media coming at ya to have a single voice, ya know? Something very simple. Basically it's an unplugged gig. I like being able to just walk in there and bring it all with me ... not have to bring in the band and all this artillery, just kinda come in and bring it in on your own."

Uh-huh. Did it evolve for you, or how did it evolve for you to include more humor in your stories and whatnot?

HR: "Well, I think it was me becoming more relaxed onstage. I was able to bring more of myself into it, whereas before I think I had some insecurities, so I had to, you know, only show one element of myself up there, and over the years I was able to bring in more ... and bring more of myself to the stage."

Uh-huh. A follow-up question: What kind of fears did you face initially, and what kind of fears do you face today when doing a solo spoken word performance, as opposed to music?

HR: "Fear? Not really fear ..."

Like trepidation or ...

HR: "Um ... well that I'll bomb, ya know... That I'll walk out there and have nothing to say. Those are some of those weird things I have in my sleep, I think about that ... Or walking out there and there's nobody there. And um... those kinda run through my mind. Or that I just won't ... It'll be like 7:55 p.m. and I won't want to do it."

Uh-huh.

HR: "But usually by about 7 p.m. I'm backstage, and there's no place I'd rather be, and nothing else I'd rather be doing than that show that night, so it always works out fine."

How much do you travel from ahh ... what you plan on saying, how much of that is impromptu, or how loose does it get up there on the spoken word thing?

HR: "Well it depends, I mean um ... this year I talked a lot about, ya know ... turning forty because I just did, and a lot of different elements came into that, and if I'm in a country for long enough, then I'll start dealing with a lot of local issues ... like I'll be in Australia for like a month at a time and a few shows in, ya know ... I've gotten ahold of what's been going on in the news there. They're very awesome."

Uh-huh.

HR: "Ya know, kind of follow certain politicians, I love to jump on and kick. And um ... so the show will start adopting a local flavor after a while, and I leave a lot up to the night. I let the evening take its course."

Uh-huh. That's cool. Australia is a wonderful place. I've been there a few times.

HR: "Yeah, it's beautiful there."

I noticed the news sometimes is ... like super-local. Like I remember hearing a news report on the radio that like a fire had happened, and the owner of Harley Davidson was damaged, like that was ...

HR: "Yeah, their news is real small, and they haven't bought into that huge media thing like America. But they will eventually."

Uh-huh.

HR: "It's a very parallel country to America. You can really watch them kind of get Americanized. It's a country that is developing really fast. You can just kind of watch it go. I'm there, like, every eleven months or so, or less. I was just there a few months ago; I'll be there in about two months from now. You can just kinda watch it advance leaps and bounds. It kinda reminds you of America, ya know, a country that has a lot of power, but has not really been around all that long."

Right, how was it, were you there near the Olympics last summer?

HR: "No, I very wisely stayed out. I try to stay out of any country that has the Olympics in it. It travels really hard, hotels are really hard, venues are really hard.

HR: "Security and police are really intense, and if you're rock 'n' roll, you just don't want to be around that kind of intensity. I learned that in the '80s when I was in the band Black Flag. The Olympics came to L.A., and we just made sure that we were well out of there before that came, and we were out of there long after it left."

Yeah, I was there that summer, and it shocked a lot of people because it wasn't as bad as they had predicted.

HR: "It was always bad for a band like us, so we didn't want to take a chance."

Well, I read in one of your bios that studio work was always a pain, and your reward always being that you get to go on tour. For a lot of bands, it's the opposite; they love to go in the studio and record, but touring is a pain for them. The ins and outs of the road ...

HR: "I guess those are different folks ..."

Is it still that way for you? What do love about touring?

HR: "I get to go out and do it, ya know? You get to go see the world, and hit the stage and rock out. Get the sweat going, be with all those people ... it's amazing."

How does an American punk icon, if I can call you that ...

HR: "You can call me anything you want."

How do you deal with the celebrity status?

HR: "I get recognized a lot, but it's usually really casual. It's all how you see it yourself. I mean, if I walked around with a lot of attitude, then I would get a lot of attitude. I, ya know, I go to hardware stores (and) buy that crap that you patch your roof with, I go patch my roof, ya know? So there I am loading that tar (expletive) into my trunk and, 'Hey, Henry Rollins, you're at a hardware store. I can't believe it!' I'm like ... 'It's the closest hardware store to where I live,' so ... that's the way I perceive myself, and it kinda calms people down when they start doing that freak out thing when they're meeting you. If you're like, 'Well, yeah ... how are you doing?' They see that you're not seeing yourself as a big deal, and they kinda stop freaking out."

Are you still trying to handle what happened to Joe Cole?

HR: "Ahh ... that's not anything we're going into, pal."

Okay. Why did you go to Jerusalem, and why was that important to you?

HR: "It wasn't all that important to me to go to Jerusalem. I had two days off in Tel Aviv, ahh ... or two days off before a show in Tel Aviv, and so I hired this tour guide to put me in this car and show me Israel. So ahh ... one of the places we went was Jerusalem, which was fascinating because I really know nothing ... well, knew nothing about any of that stuff. I'm not religious, and um ... it was just an interesting trip. Jerusalem was a beautiful place; it doesn't look like any place I've ever been to ... that's for sure."

Cool. I just saw the move *The Body* with Antonio Banderas; I don't know if you've seen that or not?

HR: "No."

I just watched it about a week ago, it's pretty awesome. Jerusalem is definite a hot spot.

HR: "Yeah, I had a good time in Israel. I mean, um ... I'm sure I didn't see but a fraction of it, but ... my experience ... I'd love to go back. It was amazing."

That's cool, what does Jesus Christ mean to you?

HR: "Nothing, not really. He was ... if He was for real, He seems ahh ... From what I've read and what I heard, it seems like He'd probably be a pretty cool guy."

Uh-huh. What do you think about his claims to be, "the Way, the Truth, and the Life; no one comes to the Father but by Me?"

HR: "That's just what somebody wrote in a book, ya know? Just like Mark Twain wrote in a book so, I don't know ... Whatever."

Uh-huh.

HR: "If it works for you, if it gets you through the night, great. If you try and make it get me through my night, then we'll have problems."

Right. Controlling people is not the name of the game.

HR: "Not mine."

Everybody probably has a sense of justice ... There are a lot of screwed up things going on in the world. What things do you care to comment on that you are doing to, uh, kinda bring justice to any particular part of the world?

HR: "Well, I try and raise consciousness at the talking shows. And, uh, I make donations to agencies that I think are doing a good thing. You know, I contribute money. And, uh, no ... small amount of it. And that's about as ... about as much as I do actively."

Uh-huh. Do they have very much connection to the music? You mentioned that you raise consciousness at the spoken shows. What about the music shows, and the albums, and liner notes, and stuff like that?

HR: "Ahh ... the songs are mainly blues songs, so there's not much politic going on there."

If you could put any lineup together to form a band, uh ... what players do you think you'd pick?

HR: "I'm in that band."

Cool. That's a great feeling.

HR: "Nowhere I'd rather be than with these guys. We're having a great time."

Good deal. Um ... how do you think that being on the Vans Warped Tour will differ from being on a headlining tour?

HR: "That's a very short ... Hence our brief stay on the Warped Tour."

Uh-huh. Do you get a lot of musicians that come up to you and talk about what an impact Black Flag had on them, and kind of honor you with what you've accomplished in the past?

HR: "Ahh ... that's happened ... But I don't really hang out with musicians really."

Uh-huh.

HR: "I don't really go out of my way to meet people, so um … yeah, I've heard that before. Um … but it kinda goes in one ear and out the other."

So, what's the future hold for your band for the next year and a half?

HR: "We'll be on tour until August of next year."

Do you travel in a van, bus, plane?

HR: "Ahh … today's a van … We're playing tonight, so it's a van. Then we're meeting up with a bus in Virginia, I guess, for the first Warped Tour, and we're going to be in a bus for the rest of it. And, you know, sometimes in Japan, you take the train to gigs, and in Australia you do a lot of flying just because the places are kind of far apart."

Right, like going from Perth to Melbourne.

HR: "Uh-huh."

It's quite a chasm. Um … How involved do you get with the songwriting process and the musical process?

HR: "Well, a lot of times I write the tunes … I write all the lyrics and sometimes the music too, and I produce the record, so I'm pretty deeply involved."

Cool. What all instruments do you play?

HR: "I don't play anything."

So, do you come up with music in your head? Do you hum stuff?

HR: "Uh-huh. Yeah, I hum the bass line to the bass player, the melody line to the guitar player, and hum the beats to the drummer."

Great. How did your DVD release come out?

HR: "Uh ... in a plastic box. (laughs) What do you mean?"

I mean was it, uh ... Has it been successful?

HR: "Sales wise? Yeah, it's sold a (expletive)."

Cool.

HR: "It's like that's one way of looking at success. I'm just glad that we got it out, because one of the shows it was set for releasing never got released, so it was sitting in the can for, like, nine years."

Wow.

HR: "So *that* I was really happy about that coming out finally. So, that to me was the real success was getting that unearthed and out there."

What um ... What do you hope to accomplish, uh ... from a historical perspective when you're said and done with music?

HR: "Ahh ... I never think about stuff like that. I just, uh, want to make good music, play good shows, and, uh, write clearly and honestly, and when I'm done, I'm done. As far as how it will be looked at, I don't really care."

Uh-huh.

HR: "It doesn't really matter in fifty years what some corny rock critic is gonna say about it, you know, it doesn't really matter to me."
Right. How, uh ...

HR: "I just reckon all that stuff will take care of itself somehow, and I will have really no say in it, so when you don't have a say in it, why bother concerning yourself with it?"

Yeah, I don't know anybody who's changed the world who's actually wanted to change the world.

HR: "Yeah, I think anyone who really went out and changed things was so busy trying to do their thing. I think anyone who says, 'I'm going to go out and change the world ... it's kind of an empty statement."

Uh-huh. How involved do the spoken and the band performances get on a tour? I mean, do you strictly do one or the other, or do you mix it up?

HR: "Oh no, you never mix 'em up, no. No ... Two totally different ways of traveling, ways of thinking. Um ... two days ago we just finished a solid month of band practice. I've been doing very hard physical training, and uh ... you know, at peak shape, and we're ready to go. There's no such preparation for a talking tour. There's no practice."

[Originally printed in November/December '01 Issue #92]

"The work's already been done by Christ to get to heaven, and by not accepting, that's what gets you into hell."

—Alice Cooper

{

14

One of God's greatest gifts to creation has to be the sense of humor. It gets us through hard times and lifts the heart when it slips into depression. I wonder if Jesus ever pulled pranks on His disciples. Having the Apostle Peter fetch a coin from a fish's mouth, for example, was probably pretty funny. Vincent Furnier, who created and plays the musical character of Alice Cooper, wishes more people got the joke. Even after decades of escalated "shock rock" that goes way beyond Cooper's horror shtick, many casual observers still look at Cooper's macabre image and react with the alarm of a concerned parent in the midst of danger. Perhaps the "don't take it too seriously" attitude of the recent Residence Inn TV commercials will cause more folks to lighten up in their assessment of Alice Cooper, who, contrary to the song, really is a nice guy.

How is your handicap in your golf game?

AC: "You know, I'm actually playing better than my handicap right now. I'm a 6 handicap, but I've been shooting right around 4. I'm trending down. I've just been playing very steady recently. I've got all the big tournaments coming up, so I don't really want to be playing really well ... right now it's okay to play really good, but I need about two weeks of really playing horrible before the tournament, and then take a week off and then come back in fresh. You never want to go into those tournaments thinking you're playing good."

Does being fresh really make a difference?

AC: "Yeah, it really does. I play almost six times a week. Sometimes, after church on Sunday, my son and I will go out and play 9 if there's nothing else going on, so sometimes seven times a week. But, the deal is, if you play that much, sometimes you get really sloppy. You start getting to the point where you forget. You're playing so much that you're just going through the motions without really playing. So, sometimes it's good to go ahead and take three or four days off, forget all about it, and come back in to the game."

I guess that's really a different level.

AC: "It really is. You have to get away from it for a while."

How involved were you with the 5.1 Surround mix of the *Billion Dollar Babies* DVD Audio?

AC: "Well, you know, I'm not technically right there with all that stuff. I, honestly, to me, I'm the writer, and I'm a little bit old school when it comes to that. I believe that more bands today need to spend more time learning how to write, rather than worrying about the techno part of this thing. You've got engineers and producers that know all that stuff. The guy that's actually playing the guitar or writing the lyrics should spend a lot more time sitting around trying to work a melody line in a lyric together, just with a pad and paper and a small little tape recorder. That's really where the songs come from. I hear too many bands today that are ... they write good riffs, but I mean, a lot of it's based on pure anger or frustration or angst. Maybe it has a good chorus, and I go, 'Yeah, but a song is not just a good chorus. You've gotta have a good chorus, you've gotta have a good B-section.' When young bands come to me and say, 'What should we do?' I say, 'Well, you've got a great look. You've got a great attitude. You've got this, this ...' I listen to the music and I go, 'Where are the songs?'

AC: "'Well, here, this one's called 'I Hate My Mother,' and this one's called 'Blah, blah, blah ...' And I say, 'I understand that you're angry. Even if you're angry, at least write a good song about being angry. Don't just scream it at me. After a while I get a little tired of being yelled at.'"

How do you feel about the outcome? Have you played it on a 5.1 Surround system?

AC: "Oh yeah, it sounds great! But I expect it to. That's what these guys are paid to do. These guys are paid to sit down and really make these things sound great. I'm glad that *that's* not my job, though. I'm glad that my job is writing the material and recording it, and not making it sound good. A lot of bands I know ... Frank Zappa was very much into the technical thing of it. I think a lot of bands do get involved in that. That's not necessarily the point. The point is to write a good song and let those guys take care of that."

Do you feel like the *Brutally Live* DVD captured the Alice Cooper live show?

AC: "Yeah, as much as it can. I mean, I don't really think, when you're trying to put the sound of a huge guitar that you hear onstage or the drums that you hear onstage—or just the powerful way it sounds onstage—when you're trying to get that through an eight-inch speaker in a car, you're never gonna catch that. So, as well as you can, I think that they catch it. I think that they do okay. You're never ever gonna catch that bigness. You're kind of confined to these speakers. In fact, when we used to mix a record, we would never listen to a record through the big JBL's and all these great big woofers and tweeters and everything. We would mix the record and then play it through a two-inch or four-inch car speaker one. 'What does it sound like through there?' Because that's what people are going to be hearing. The technical guys are really good at that. We don't get much involved. I hear it onstage, of course, and I can hear if something's wrong or out of balance, and I'll go over and say, 'You know what? That guitar is so distorted that we're missing the point. I want it to be distorted, but I don't want it to be so distorted that we miss the point of this thing. I still want to hear the notes.'"

Have you received any feedback from the mothers of those boy band members that you blew up in the "Gimme" video?

AC: (laughs) "No, but I understand that the band is still together. The fact is they actually were a boy band. They were trying to be a boy band. They had a very good sense of humor about it. I told him, 'You know, everyone is trying to be The Backstreet Boys. Everybody is trying to be *NSYNC.' I said, 'What about a gothic boy band?' I said, 'Nobody's done that. This silliness that we put you in, with this goth thing, may actually be a great look. It's certainly better than that candy-coated thing that they do.' I know The Backstreet Boys and I know *NSYNC, and they're very, very professional. These guys are very good at what they do. They rehearse more than we do, and we rehearse a lot. I give them a lot of credit. I'm not crazy about the music at all. It's not my kind of music, but I give them a lot of credit for being professional."

I read a recent interview with you, where you talked about taking your band to see those bands, just to show them how hard working they are and how tight they perform.

AC: "Yeah. There is such a thing as, you know, you get a lot of the metal bands, a lot of the alternative bands, and the goth bands, and they've got this great attitude, and you get onstage, and they're one-dimensional. I tell them, 'You know what? You could do ten different things. The first band like you that takes it three or four different levels is gonna do really well.' But, you know, they don't wanna work at it. They would rather just do what's expected. You get up; you jump up and down. You do the hip-hop thing up and down. And you do that one move that every single one of those bands make, and you're happy with that. I say, 'I don't know. I wouldn't be satisfied with that. I would take it another step.' But that's what the Alice Cooper show has always been. We've always taken it the next step."

How did these recent TV commercials come about, and how have you felt about the process and the outcome?

AC: "Well, the funny thing about it is—I've always liked the idea of injecting Alice into places he doesn't belong. In the early days, Alice was, without the nastiness ... I was the Marilyn Manson of that day. Or now you could say, 'Marilyn Manson is the Alice Cooper of his day.' The difference was that Alice Cooper had a sense of humor. I mean, the things that I did, they were never political. They were never religious. They were never anything. Mine was all pure schlock horror, comedy, and rock 'n' roll. It was pretty harmless compared to what's going on now. So, I always liked the idea that Alice was Americana. He was an American, sort of, character that people totally ... Now—ten, thirty years later, now I'm Americana. I'm a piece of the fabric of America, as much as Bob Hope is. Or anybody like that. So, I think that Alice being in the middle of suburbia chastising a guy for cutting his lawn and not taking his kids to the park is a funny idea. I think that it's actually such a juxtaposition, a strange juxtaposition, that Alice is being the one that's sort of being the establishment guy, saying, 'Hey! Get off your butt and take your kids to a ball game or something ...' I like that idea."

I think America likes it too. Everybody I've heard that's seen it just loves it.

AC: "Well, it does make a point. I think that people ... now that people know I am Christian and now that people know that I am a dad and a father, the Alice character is a character that I play—the same way that if I were playing Dracula or if I was playing The Joker, or if I was playing Mingna Merciless, or any of these characters ... It's a character that I play onstage, and when I leave the stage, he stays there. I go home and, you know, take the kids to the basketball game and take my little girl to ballet class. I always tell people, 'I'm Fred McMurray offstage and Bela Ligosi onstage.'"

A lot of your music has had the appearance of being somewhat autobiographical in nature. Take the *From The Inside* era, for example. And the trilogy you wrote that began with *The Last Temptation* seemed to mimic this trait as well. What kind of price have you paid or benefits have you seen from freely sharing a part of yourself in your art?

AC: "Well, I think that a writer—especially a lyric writer—is always going to be confessing at all times. No matter what he does, he's always going to be talking about what he thinks, what he believes. Even if it's in irony, if it's in story, if it's in whatever—you're always revealing a lot about yourself.

"*From The Inside* was definitely written about my alcoholism. *The Last Temptation* to me was a good storyline, because it was about a kid that was offered everything ... And, of course, it was a parallel of Christ being tempted in the wilderness. But this kid gets offered everything. You think, 'Well, he's going to buy into it. He's going to join this guy's circus.' And the circus, of course, is like a synonym for the world. The showman was a synonym for a satanic thing. So, this guy's offering him sex, women, money, fame, and the catch at the end of it is the kid doesn't buy into it.

"I was trying to make the point that you don't have to buy into it. I was trying to make the point that, Hollywood tells you, 'If you're fifteen and you haven't been laid yet and you're not high all the time, then there's something wrong with you.' I think that's the worst message that you can give a kid. He's got all his life to deal with that. Why are we forcing him into all these heavy things when he's fourteen? Well, it's because it makes money. That album in particular was saying, 'Don't buy into it. You don't have to.' In fact, you're the hero when you don't buy into it. Now, for Alice Cooper to be saying that, it obviously makes people that were Alice Cooper fans before kind of take a step backwards and say, 'Wait a minute! This is the same Alice Cooper that was selling sex, death, and money!'

"And I'm like, 'Exactly, but I'm not him anymore. Now Alice ... there's a change of heart. There's a change of what I believe. Now I'm telling you, with more authority, that you don't have to buy into that.' And when they say, 'How dare you!' I go, 'Well, you know, I'm not going to sell as many albums doing this, but I don't care about that. The fact is, there may be some kids out there that listen to that and go, 'Wow, good. The pressure's off. Now I don't have to go try to get laid every weekend. Or, I don't have to try to get stoned just so I can be part of the guys. I can be like Alice. I can do what Alice does.' And really, it's not what I'm saying, it's what Christ said! I'm just trying to echo what He would want you to do. But it's funny that I have to use the Alice Cooper character to get that point across.

"The funny thing was that *The Last Temptation* really wasn't part of the trilogy. That was on its own. That was the first thing I wrote as a Christian. And then, it was six years before I wrote *Brutal Planet*. *Brutal Planet* was a whole different story. *Brutal Planet* was a story that was talking about, 'What's the world like? Let's get a picture of the future fifty years from now, when all of the systems have failed—church, family, school, politics, every system has failed, and there's no God. Let's say that no one believes in God. Well, what have we got? Now we've got *Brutal Planet*—this horrible place that nobody wants to be. That's what that album was about. *Dragontown* was part two of that, which was a little bit more character driven. I was kind of like showing you characters that are there. The point on that one is, 'You can even be a nice guy and be in hell. The road to hell is littered with nice guys with good intentions.' Part three is in the works right now."

Any hints or directions you're going to take there?

AC: "Well, I think I'm going to solidify the fact that once you're there, you're there. You don't work your way out of hell. You don't work your way into heaven, and you don't work your way out of hell. The work's already been done by Christ to get to heaven, and by not accepting, that's what gets you into hell. And so, that's not going to be a popular thing, either. But, you know, it's really not my job to make it popular. It's my job to make a great sounding album and to make people go, 'Wow! What a cool album!' And then when they start listening to it, they get the message."

I think you've done a really good job on the last two.

AC: "Well, thanks. I surprised people, because it was as heavy as Rob Zombie. It was as heavy as any of these bands that are out there, and they're all friends of mine. So, when they heard this album, they were going, 'Oh man! Alice is really heavy, and he's right there with us.' I think when they heard the message on it, they were a little taken back, because of the fact that it sounds like it's going to be selling something else. Then, when they hear it, they go, 'Wow! This is a heavy album that's selling something good.'"

I'm not concluding here, but I want to say that I am grateful for your time today.

AC: "Oh, thanks a lot. I'm glad that we finally got to talk!"

Yeah, me too. I'm honored to do the interview. I've been pursuing it for a couple years now. I was happy to get a call from your wife to set it up ...

AC: "Oh yeah, she's great! My wife is great. Twenty-five years ..."

Congratulations. That leads me to ask, 'Are there any unusual circumstances or motivations that made you want to do this interview?'

AC: "You know, first of all, I do mostly the secular rock. But I think ... My pastor feels the same way. I am not necessarily praise rock. I'm not Christian praise music. I think that I go to a different place. And I think that Christianity needs to go much more into the secular arts. I think that we need to be heard not just by Christians. I mean, it's nice ... bands like Creed, P.O.D. There's some bands out there that are saying some pretty good things. And then there's a lot of really good praise rock bands. I've just never felt ... I do that in church. I do that in prayer. I do that, but I think that my message is more of a warning. I don't mind being the prophet of doom. I think that that's more fitted for what Alice is. I feel that, if God is going to use Alice Cooper, it's going to be more on a level of a warning. It's not going to be on a level of, 'Isn't everything great? Isn't everything good? Aren't we all wonderful?' Alice is going to be more like, 'Be careful! Satan is not a myth. Don't sit around pretending like Satan is just a joke.' Because I have a lot of friends that do believe that. I think my job is to warn about Satan."

I can't remember which came first for me: hearing rumors that Alice Cooper was saved, or seeing a decided turn of morality in songs like "Hey Stoopid."

AC: "Yeah. That was a pre-Christian song. That was a song that was basically ... I think there was something going on in my heart then, because here it was a lot of kids committing suicide. And I was thinking, 'How do you talk to a friend?' Doug, if you and I had known each other for a hundred years, you and I are buddies since high school, and this ... And you're

going, 'Hey Alice, I'm going to go put a gun to my head.' How would I talk
to you? I wouldn't say, 'Doug, my son, don't do that.' I'd go, 'Hey stupid,
what are you talking about?' You know, you would call your buddy stupid.
You would say, 'Jerk! What are you? Out of your mind?' I know you have
friends that you talk to like that. It's an endearing thing. What I was doing
was, I was talking to those guys, my whole fanclub out there, and calling
them ... just going, 'Hey stoopid! What are you doing? What are you talking
about? You're going to kill yourself? Because your girlfriend left you, or
you're going to kill yourself because your boyfriend is cheating on you?' I
was trying to make a point that you've got to talk to people on their level.
I'm not going to shake a finger in your face and go, 'Now, now, now! Don't
do that!' Your parents are going to do that. Alice Cooper's not your parents.
Alice is there. He's your friend. And he's going to talk to you as a friend
would."

Well, what is your story? I'd like to know how you came to know Christ and,
if you want to, sprinkle it with any timelines that might be relevant.

AC: "Well, you have to remember that my grandfather was an evangelist for
sixty years. I grew up in the Church. I grew up in a Protestant church, a very
strong Bible-believing church. I was in church on Wednesday nights, Friday
nights, all day Sunday. All my friends were church kids, and I was very
happy. In high school, all of a sudden, The Beatles came along. I saw a way
for me to basically express myself. I was going to be an artist of some sort. I
didn't want to work at Safeway. I didn't want to work with my dad at
drafting or anything like that. So, we put a band together just to make some
money on the weekends, not realizing that it was going to develop into
something that was going to end up being a life work—thirty-five years later,
I'm still doing this. I think that it's almost like winning the lottery—is
getting a break in this business. Unfortunately, along with that break comes
all the things you don't see. You don't see the alcoholism coming. You don't
see the sin that comes with it. I don't think I went out there in the world and
said, 'Boy! I can't wait to get out there and sin.' A lot of my lyrics, even from
the very beginning, you could tell there was a lot of Christianity in those
lyrics, or at least there was some knowledge of the Bible. But I got caught up
in it, just like anything else. You know, fame, money, power. And I invented
a character that a lot of people thought was satanic. I never, ever once

thought Alice was satanic. I always looked at Alice as being much more funny than that. And, even in those days, I was very insulted if somebody said, 'satanic.' I always thought, 'That's really not what I believe in at all. I still believe in God. I still believe in Christ,' but I wasn't a committed Christian. My dad was a pastor, so it was probably hard on him, even though he was a music fan. He didn't mind the music. He just didn't like what came with it.

"But, about ... let me see, 1985, '86, '89, '90 ... I had been wrestling. I had been going to church with my wife. Her dad's a pastor. We almost broke up, because of the drinking. I had an alcoholic problem. Finally we went with a counselor—a Christian counselor—and we decided to start going to church together. And I went to this church where there was this pastor—Reverend Jackson—that was one of those hellfire pastors. He was not ... There was 6,000 people in the room, and he was always talking directly to me. I would be hidden somewhere up in the 500th row, crouched down, and what he was saying was hitting me right between the eyes—was hitting me right in the heart, right in the soul. God was speaking to me. I would squirm every Sunday I was sitting there. I would tell Cheryl when I'd leave, 'I'm never going back there again.' Of course, the next Sunday I was back there, because I knew that what he was saying was right. I think that I became a Christian, initially, more out of the fear of God, rather than the love of God. I truly did believe that He was in control of my destiny, my eternal destiny. I did not want to go to hell. And I became a Christian, I think, out of fear. But I think fear, you know what they say, is the beginning of knowledge. The fear of God is the beginning of knowledge. When I started, you know, really understanding Christianity, that's when I started becoming more in love with Christ. I think that that's an ongoing process. I think that you don't just fall in love with Christ and that's it. I think that you learn to love Him more all the time. So, I'm still in that process of learning more and learning to love more. But, it was definitely ... my initial thing was out of the fear of God. I didn't want to be standing in front of God ... an angry God. I would much rather stand in front of an angry Satan than an angry God. And when I realized that, I said, 'Well, then I better be on the right side here. I better be on the side where Christ is my lawyer. When my life ends, I want Christ to say, 'No, he's one of Mine,' and be washed in that blood, rather than washed in any other blood.' So, that's basically where I am today. It's an ongoing thing. Being a Christian is something you just progress in. You just keep progressing. You learn. You go to your Bible studies. You pray. And it's not always easy, because there's so many things in the world that pull you away. But I think it's an ongoing thing. What God's expecting us to do... What Christ is expecting us to do, is just keep going. Just keep the faith, and just keep it going."

That's cool. I think I can really relate, because my story's kind of a prodigal son story, but initially I came to Christ as an eleven-year-old back in '74, and I think I came forward at an altar call, probably, at one of those hellfire and brimstone sermons. Back then it was based around, "The rapture's gonna happen, and you better be right with God, or you'll be left behind ..."

AC: "Right, where if everyone disappears except you ...

Yeah, then you're in trouble, bud. Well, you have seemingly avoided the Christian celebrity, "Let's get him on the *700 Club* mentality." And my question is: Where did you acquire the wisdom to make that astute decision?

AC: "I have been surrounded by guys that are strong Christian guys. A youth pastor, my pastor, and all of them have protected me. They've all said, 'You know, it's great who you are. Be careful of celebrity Christianity,' because it's really easy to use somebody. It's really easy to focus on Alice Cooper and not on Christ. It's so embarrassing in the very beginning, when somebody would say, 'We want you to speak at our youth thing.' And you get there and it says, 'ALICE COOPER' in huge letters, 'speaking about Christ' in small letters. And I'm sitting there going, 'That is blasphemy—the fact that my name is even bigger.' That tells me something right there that something's wrong. I'm a rock singer. I'm nothing more than that. I'm not a politician; I'm not a philosopher. We all have our ideas on what's going on in the world. I'm not a politician. I'm a rock singer. I can find clever little ways of saying it. I can sing, and I can act and do all this—things to make you laugh, smile, cringe, and do all those things, but that's all I am. What I really am is a follower of Christ. This is my job. I always tell people, 'My job is rock 'n' roll. My life is dedicated to follow Christ. So, don't look to me as being some ...' When I do go to speak to people, they think I'm going to have some answers. I go, 'I don't have any answers. Please, give me some answers.

I can give you what I think. I think that the most important thing that I know is dependence on Christ. That's all I know, is that I have absolutely no answers, and I have no power. I can entertain you, but when it comes to being subject to Christ, I consider myself low on the totem pole of knowledgeable Christians. So, don't look for answers from me. Look for encouragement. I'll encourage you, but I can't sit around telling you, giving you any biblical answers.'

"I think that sometimes celebrity Christianity, they confuse us, like we know more than anyone else. Like we know something that you don't know. I study the same Bible you do. I listen to the same Sunday school or listen to the same pastors. I am just as ... I am in the same boat as anybody. Now, if it comes to music or staging, yeah, okay, I've got a leg up on everybody on that. But when it comes to being a Christian, then that's something we have to deal with every day."

That's awesome. It seems like the mentality out there is that God needs celebrities to endorse His product, which is ridiculous.

AC: "It's just absurd. First of all, God doesn't need our help at all. I run a big celebrity charity thing called Solid Rock Foundation. And we always have to remind ourselves that God doesn't need for us to raise $200,000. If God wanted us to have $200,000, there would be a check in the mail, and we would open it up and it would be there. God is more interested in our process of how we raise it. He's interested in our time. He's interested in our attitude, our ethics. It's not the amount at the end of the day. It's how we got there, how we represented Him. To me, I think that's why you do these things. It's not how much money we raise."

I don't have any statistics, but I would venture to say that various chemical addictions plague millions of people. Do you think these types of addictions ever lose their grip on people or temptations ever go away?

AC: "Especially now, I would not want to be a teenager right now. Even though, in some ways, teenagers are more informed now than they were when I was a kid ... We thought marijuana was absolutely harmless. We thought, 'Well, this is harmless, and that's harmless, and a couple of beers can't hurt ya.' If I were actually, this may be a startling thing for me to say, and maybe ... after being an alcoholic for years ... If I were going to outlaw something, drug-wise, the first thing I would outlaw would be alcohol. If you look at your statistics, 90 percent of fatal car accidents are alcohol. Almost 90 percent of homicides have to do with alcohol, especially spousal ... You don't hear of a lot of people smoking grass getting aggressive. Of course, I'm against all addictions. I'm against all things ... But I think alcohol is the most harmful—out of everything that I've been around. And that's the legal thing. It's odd that cigarettes and alcohol, the two most destructive things, are the most legal. Seven percent of heroin addicts die of heroin. 85 or 90 percent of alcoholics die of alcohol. Alcohol is legal. I don't get it."

It always seemed kind of hypocritical to a young mind ...

AC: "It's unbelievable."

How has your personal experience shaped your views on sin, our sinful nature, and how you relate to others that are struggling with such addictions?

AC: "Well, it's like anything else, I've got gay friends. I've got friends that are in bad relationships that are sleeping with ... that are certainly not married, that are sleeping together. And, you know, I'm not standing in their face, wagging my finger in their face. If they ask me, I say ... I've had a gay friend that's gone to me and said, 'Is being gay a sin?' And I go, 'Yeah. Do I hate you because you're gay? No. Are you one of my best friends? In fact, I think you're such a good person. I think you made a bad choice here, that I'm going to tell you why. It's not me saying this. If you believe in the Bible at all, let me show you where it says that. Let me show you where it says it's an abomination. Let me show you where it says that God is not going to allow that in heaven. That's a sin that He looks really badly on.' You know, I could take him to the Bible and show him where that's specific. But I don't write songs about it. I haven't felt that *that's* something I should write about now. Maybe if I do, I will. I'm not a homophobic.

"I have lots of friends that are gay. I have lots of friends that are in a lot of bad situations. And, just because I'm a Christian doesn't mean that I don't have to deal with sin every single day. I mean, I'm just as deep in it as anybody else. We all have to deal with it. It's not going to go away. Now, it's understanding that we're a new person in Christ and that we're not a slave to it. That's really something that we have to deal with it."

I think that's one of the things you made loud and clear on *The Last Temptation*: that you weren't a slave to the devil anymore.

AC: "I think that's important. And I think that's something to be joyous about and happy about. But it's still something we better be very careful about. Because he's not going to say, 'Well, I give up on Alice.' Or he's not going to say, 'Well, that Doug's such a good guy. I'm just going to give up on him.' In fact, he's going to focus on you a little better. He's going to start finding the little things that you didn't think he knew about. And he's going to go, 'Hey, I see a little crack in the armor here. I'm going to go there. He's never going to go where you're strong. He's going to go where you're weak.'"

Without naming names, of course, have you had the opportunity to pull anyone from the fire, so to speak, and if so, how rewarding was that?

AC: "Well, I don't know. A lot of times, I've had a couple of people that were friends of mine that I've talked to that have vocally said they have. Sometimes you have to just kind of wait and see if it's fruitful or not. I have talked to some big stars about this, some really horrific characters, without naming names, like you said. And you'd be surprised. The ones that you would think are the furthest gone, are the ones that are more apt to listen. Because they've done every drug. They've done every girl. They've had every car. They've had everything there is to fill up that hole that they can't fill. All of a sudden, when they come to me and they go, 'Alice, what is this with you, this Christian thing? You're happily married. You seem to be happy with everything. You don't have any enemies. What's going on with this?'

"I look at that as being an opportunity to say, 'Look. You knew me before. You know me now. I was miserable when I was an alcoholic. I was huge. We were voted the biggest band in the world. Voted #1 band in the world. Was I happy? No. I tried to find that happiness through alcohol and through everything else. Now, would I want to go back and be the number one band in the world and forget what I have now? No, I wouldn't change this for anything.'

"They don't understand that. I say, 'What you don't understand is the peace of mind I have—the peace I have in my heart, that I didn't have before.' If God has opened their ears at all to hear that, it plants a seed, and later on, you never know, it may be fruition. It may work. It may be something. But again, that's really for God to open their ears. Nobody's gonna hear what I'm saying until God opens their ears—that's the miracle. I mean, I could talk myself blue in the face about what's happened to me, and they're just gonna look at me and go, 'So what?' But if God says something ... if God opens up a little crack there, then it might not just be, 'So what,' but it may be, 'I wanna hear a little bit more about that.' Those are the guys that I know there's something going on with."

It goes back to that whole thing, "If Marilyn Manson got saved, just think about how many people would just flock to Christ!" I don't think so.

AC: "Yeah. I've been saved, and there's not people flocking to Christ because I'm saved. It doesn't work like that. Yeah, people are interested in it, and people are kinda intrigued by it. I think the best testimony that I can have is to lead a Christian life. And I tell people that all the time. 'You know, just because I'm a rock 'n' roller, doesn't mean I have to lead a rock 'n' roll lifestyle.' That's the difference. I can be in the enemy camp and not buy into what they sell. But, again, nobody's going to listen until God opens their ears to hear."

Speaking of lifestyles, your experience has definitely given you friendships and alliances with many a partying star. If I asked you to dispel some of the mythology around famous rock 'n' roll celebrities, what would be some of your main points in doing so?

AC: "Oh, I think ... See, what you hear are urban legends. I'd say 80 percent of the mystique of Alice Cooper was based on urban legends. Frank Zappa, for one, never got high. Frank Zappa used to drink coffee and smoke cigarettes. People used to think, 'Well, he was the biggest stoner since Cheech & Chong.' No. He never got high. When you think of these other ones, especially if you have a really theatrical personality or image, people expect or will believe the worst. People would believe anything they heard about Alice Cooper because of what we look like. Certainly, at that time, we didn't discourage any of that! We said, 'Great! The more crude rumors about Alice, the better!' And now, of course, I laugh about them and go, 'No, none of that happened. That didn't happen ...' They want to believe that about me, Ozzy, Marilyn Manson. I guarantee you that 80 percent of the things you've heard about Marilyn Manson are not ... are just things you've heard. He knows what he's doing on a level of button-pushing. He knows how to push the right buttons to make parents mad. That's how you get kids to love you. If they're fifteen and their parents hate you, then they're going to love you."

Speaking of celebrities, is it true that you have a friendship with RC Sproule?

AC: "Oh yeah. RC is one of my heroes. When I first became a Christian, I went to a few of the retreats, and I just love to hear him talk. I loved his books. His books for me were really good, because they were written so that I could understand them, and they were practical. I understand practical Christianity. I love to read things that I can apply to my life. Then I met him, we played golf together, and I just really liked him. And I think he really liked me, and he was intrigued by the fact that, 'Here's Alice Cooper sitting in the crowd listening to this, and he's just like everybody else. He's a new Christian that wants to know all of these answers.' He's great. He never treated me any different. Every time that they have one in town, and I go to see him, it's always good to see him. I support his ministry. I financially support Legionnaire."

A few years ago, I was reading an interview that Lonn Friend was doing with you for Pirate Radio or KROQ, and he expressed an appreciation for your art-expressed faith, while deriding the so-called preaching of Creed. Why do you think you got that reaction?

AC: "Well, again I think it was like Lonn ... Lonn is one of those guys that is very knowledgeable about the business of rock and roll. Totally on a secular level, totally understands the sexuality of it, the greed of it, everything that makes rock 'n' roll appealing to most people. And he knew me before. Then, all of a sudden, when he knows me now, and he'll say, 'I want to do an article on blah, blah, blah,' and I go, 'No, because I don't believe that anymore.' I like the fact that Lonn Friend respects that. He respects the fact that I don't believe that anymore. It makes Alice Cooper a pretty unique character—not any better than anybody, but when you've gone from being the poster boy for sin to somebody that won't do those things anymore, it really is intriguing to the average guy—especially to Lonn. I got along very well with Lonn. We did the radio show. When it got into things that I thought were getting off color or something ... I can laugh at a silly joke or even a gross joke or anything. When it gets into pornography, when it gets into things that I think are too off-color, then I start remembering, 'Hey, I'm representing Christ here.' I would back off of that and say, 'Hey guys, not on my time. If I'm going to be involved with this, we've got to stay away from that.' And, not trying to be more righteous than him, but in all reality, trying to be more righteous than him. You don't want to come off like that, but that's what we are called to do. We are called to have a conscience that we didn't have before. The nice thing is that he respects that."

It's not easy to be the party-pooper.

AC: "Not at all. I'll sit there and, if that starts coming up, I just walk away. The great thing about when Christ enters your life is the fact that He is in your heart, and all of a sudden, you realize that you shouldn't be in this place. I don't care where it is. All of a sudden, something goes on at a party, and it started out being okay, and all of a sudden there's a naked girl running around the room. All of a sudden my soul feels sick. My soul feels like, 'Hey, you don't belong in here, do you?' And I walk out. I say, 'Hey, this isn't right. I don't belong here.' Or, even I'm laying in bed at night, and I'm flipping through HBO and Showtime, and I'm a man like anybody else, and all of a sudden there's almost every sex act you can imagine on television. I think if I find myself staying a little bit too long on that station, I start getting this feeling inside of, 'Hey, what are we doing? Why are we watching this? Is this what you want to be filled up with?' And that was a conscience I didn't have before, and that to me is an evidence of Christ in my life."

The Holy Spirit working ...

AC: "I think so. We call it conscience. I call it Holy Spirit. I think it's the Holy Spirit in your life."

I agree. How do you think of some of your past work in light of your worldview? Are there any songs you choose not to perform anymore because of lyrics?

AC: "Oh yeah, tons of 'em, especially songs on the *Trash* album. There were certain songs where I was very, very clever about sexual innuendo and about, 'Go get laid as fast and as many times as you can, because it's cool,' and all that. All those different attitudes of, 'Drinking is the greatest thing, and let's get high.' Any song that has to do with that, I look back. When I put my show together, I still do twenty-six songs in the show, and I'm very careful about what the lyrics are in those songs. I don't see anything wrong with 'Eighteen.' I don't see anything wrong with, you know, sort of my declaration of independence when I'm eighteen years old and the angst involved. That's a normal thing. 'School's Out' I don't have a problem with. 'No More Mr. Nice Guy' I don't have a problem with. Some of my stuff is just fun, silly stuff. But, when it comes to things like 'Spark in the Dark,' 'Bed of Nails,' songs like that, you know, I start going, 'You know what? I can't sing that anymore. I was selling that, and now I'm not selling that.' So, I tried to write songs that were equally as good, only with a better message."

You brought up some of the urban legends before, and one of the questions I was going to ask is: How did some of these urban legends come around to you? What was the circumstances involved of how you actually heard these rumors?

AC: "Oh, well, what it is, I heard the same urban legends about Mick Jagger when he was the guy. And then when Mick Jagger wasn't the guy and Jim Morrison was the guy, then all those rumors were inherited by him. And then I got them, and then Johnny Rotten from The Sex Pistols inherited them, and then Ozzy got them, and Marilyn's got them now. It's like, if you're that bad boy of rock 'n' roll, suddenly now you are the inheritor of all of the rumors. You know, one of them has always been, 'Well, Frank Zappa took a crap onstage and Alice ate it ... a gross-out contest.' I heard that about Mick Jagger when I was in high school. That rumor is as old ... they probably said that about Frank Sinatra and Bing Crosby. That's as old as the one about the drive-in theater, where the guy goes to get popcorn, gives the girl the Spanish Fly, and comes back and she's impaled on the gear shift knob. I heard that when I was in elementary school. I just heard it recently. 'Hey dad, did you hear about the girl ...'

"'My son,' I said, 'That was old when I was in elementary school.' There are kids that want to believe that stuff. It's just amazing what kind of longevity those rumors have. I guess they were so good ... it's like a hit record. They just don't go away."

Another thing you touched on earlier that I wanted to delve into a little bit more, is: How did your parents feel about Alice Cooper's career? Did you ever sit down and give them an explanation of what it is you do and what your concepts are about?

AC: "Well, I think my dad understood my sense of humor, because I got it from him. My dad was one of those guys that was a very classy guy. Very funny guy. My dad probably could've done stand-up comedy, as well as preach. He loved music. Loved The Beatles. Thought The Beatles were great. Thought the Stones were cool. But, my dad could preach and put you on the floor. He was such a good preacher. Dead-solid right-on. He wasn't going left or right of what the Bible said. But, he would be shaving and I would test him. I'd pick up the Bible and I'd go, 'Ezekiel 7:35,' and he would go, 'The Lord saith unto me...' and he would go on. I'd say, 'Okay, Galatians 6:9,' and he would quote it, never even missing a beat.

"And then I would say, 'Who played bass for The Animals?' And he'd go, 'Chez Chandler.' I'd go, 'You know what? That's cool that my dad would know that!' He would know who Steven Tyler was. He would know who Jeff Beck was. 'Was Jeff Beck better than Jimmy Page?' (and he'd say) 'Uh, yeah, I think so. Maybe on phrasing. Maybe not on writing ...' I was really impressed with that. But, my dad would also say, 'I love the music, but I don't like what comes with it.' He would always talk to me and say, 'Vince ...' Of course, he wouldn't call me Alice. He'd say, 'Don't buy into all this stuff.' Of course, I became an alcoholic. When I quit drinking and was straight, you know, that was ... My dad always knew, I think, that I was going to be a ... like you are with the Prodigal Son. And my mom is probably still thinking that I'm going to end up being a pastor. And maybe I will. If I am, it'll be in some small little church in Northern Arizona. It won't be on *The 700 Club*."

Was the boa constrictor used onstage ever a pet? And did this image, as well as songs like "The Black Widow," ever get you in situations with fans that you'd rather not have been in? If so, explain.

AC: "Ahh, no. I mean, the snake was something that, of course, at that time, I would pick up a snake and go, 'This is frightening.' I was terrified of snakes. Somebody had one backstage at a show in Florida, and I figured, 'If I am that terrified by this three-foot boa constrictor, then what would an audience be effected by if I had about a nine- or ten-foot one around my neck?' And, of course, it worked like a charm. And everybody thought that I knew everything about snakes and that I was a snake guy. I didn't own a snake. I didn't have a pet. I got to like them as pets. Actually, they were very good pets. They were very non-violent, to be honest with you. But it repre-sented sex. It represented evil. It represented a lot of things to the audience. Of course, it just fit right in with Alice's image.

"'The Black Widow' was just something that was part of the nightmare—'Welcome To My Nightmare.' It was, 'What scares me?' I hate black widow spiders, so I'm going to write a whole song about it, and I'm going to have four black widows that are climbing up the web behind me, that are gonna be dancers. I had the means to create anything. Another thing I would've done that was a nightmare of mine—I'm needle-phobic. I just hate needles. I would have probably put giant needles coming down. You always try to write onstage things that scare you. So, 'The Black Widow' had really no ... It was just fluff. It had no philosophy. I was just trying to write something that would scare people. Getting Vincent Price to actually do it for me—to me it was funny. I saw more humor in it than horror."

How have you felt about your own mythification and the other baggage that your image and persona has attracted over the years?

AC: "Well, I understand it. I understand that every generation needs a villain. And I didn't mind being the villain. I think now people understand what my villainy ... During the '70s, if you change your name to Alice and you had a snake onstage and you got decapitated, well, the Christian Right was going to think I was anti-Christ. I had absolutely no religious ... anything religious to do with this at all. I didn't see anything wrong. I thought it was pure Vaudeville. I thought it was not any more dangerous than a Saturday afternoon horror movie—only it was done to music. But, of course, certain very strong conservative religious rights are looking for anything to, you know, tie you to that's going to make it easy for them to say, 'This is where our kids are going.' And, at the time, I can understand why I was their target—the same way I can see Marilyn Manson now. Even with Marilyn Manson, I never said I was satanic. He says he's a priest of the satanic church. That even made me mad! He even pressed my buttons, and I realized, 'Geez, if I were going to try to piss off everybody, that's what I would say.' I doubt if he is (or) has anything to do with the satanic church. But that's what I would say, I think, if I weren't a Christian; I would do something that was going to upset everybody like that.

"You know, I look at what I did back then, and I think by now people know that that was then, this is now. Hopefully, when they see me onstage now, they enjoy the fact that I'm probably as dangerous as Vincent Price or any of these Saturday matinee horror characters. I'm not trying to be evil. If I do come off as evil sometimes, I come off as psychologically unbalanced or insane. And sometimes you do have to play the devil to get the audience to believe in the devil. But I do it ... I pray before I go onstage every single time that what my ultimate message here is in glorification of God, not in any destruction of God."

I could probably explain the answer to the next question, but for the benefit of any blue-haired ladies that pick up our magazine, how would you explain your live show and its relevance to your current worldview?

AC: "Well, again, I think that my live show ... If you've gone to see David Copperfield, which I'm sure every blue-haired old lady has gone to see, he does a certain amount of illusion onstage. And it's done to rock music. And it's a show. I basically do the same thing that David Copperfield does. I do an illusion of cutting my head off. I do about four or five different illusions onstage. It's no more evil than that (spoken by carefully pronouncing each syllable). If you like David Copperfield, you should have no problem with Alice Cooper. I certainly do have a legend behind Alice Cooper, and when people say, 'Oh, go back and do this and this and this,' I go, 'No. I've done that. It was okay at the time. I've repented from a lot of things that I did back then.' Some of the things I don't think were harmful. You know, I don't see a lot of the things I did being any more harmful than Frank Sinatra. In fact, I've heard worse things come out of that. Certainly, we were never more violent than Shakespeare. If you've ever seen *Macbeth*, our show has never been more violent than a Shakespeare thing. People need to come with a different point of view ... come and see the show, and say, 'Gee, that was fun. I really liked the part when you sang, 'Cleansed by fire,' and you're sort of talking about redemption and talking about repentance. Then, a lot of my stuff is very innocuous. I think a lot of my stuff is just pure rock 'n' roll party—balloons and confetti. If you're coming to see Alice Cooper to see something that's like a sinful party, you're not going to see it. It's just not what it's about. If you wanna see that, go see Motley Crue."

What do you wish more people knew about you? And what is one question that you often wanted to be asked in an interview?

AC: "Well, I think that we covered an awful lot of that today, and I think we're going to have to make this the last question. I've got to get my son to a basketball game. But I think that people should ... If there's one thing that I'd like to dispel to the average guy that knows nothing about Alice is that Alice is, if anything, anti-satanic. There are people out there that they think of Alice Cooper ... They think of the makeup, and the first thing they think of is satanic. Well, I have to deal with that every day. Me, having to turn that around in lyrics and in interviews, has been a lifetime work. It's something that I think God's said, 'Hey, you've made this bed; now you've got to get yourself out of it.' (he laughs) I understand that, and I totally go, 'Okay,' and I take on that challenge. It's either me quitting or taking on the challenge of letting people know who I really am now. I think I bring more of a good message by telling people who I was then and who I am now. That, to me, is a very good message. It's a testimony in itself. So, for all of you who don't know who I am, listen to the last three albums, listen to the lyrics, and give me a break. (laughs)

"I think that people have got to realize ... I do know a lot of people, and I respect them, are Christians that are afraid to give out candy on Halloween. Okay, I understand that. I understand that in the old, old, old days, Halloween may have been that. To me ... I'm from Detroit. When I was a kid, you put on a costume, and you go get candy. That's about as evil as it is. But there are people with the same mentality that can't imagine a rock 'n' roller being a Christian. All I'm trying to say is, 'I was one thing at one time, and I'm something new. I'm a new creature now. Don't judge Alice by what he used to be. Praise God for what I am now.'"

Amen.

[Originally printed in March/April '02 Issue #94]

"Instead of the focus being on, you know, following your heart and about faith, it seemed like the focus was put on a certain man that happened to be speaking that day."

—Dave Williams

15

{ DROWNING POOL }

At the time of this interview, Drowning Pool was in an enviable position. They had a platinum-selling debut on Wind-up Records, a building fan base, and a mainstage slot at the coveted Ozzfest traveling metal festival. When we caught wind of a tour that was headed our way, and an opportunity for an interview with singer Dave Williams, Editor Doug Van Pelt jumped on it.

On a sad note, just months after this interview took place, Dave Williams was found dead on his tour bus in the middle of Ozzfest (August 14, 2002). He died of a heart muscle disease called Cardiomyopathy, which was never diagnosed prior to his death. His bandmates miss him dearly, and his label has since released Sinema, *a tribute documentary on Wind-up Records.*

How do you feel about playing mainstage at Ozzfest this year?

DW: "It feels good. To be at Ozzfest at all is a privilege. We had a really good time last summer, and to be a part of it this summer is great too; and to find out that we got mainstage is pretty incredible."

How do you like your new album?

DW: "I like it. I'm proud of the way it came out. I like the way it sounds. I like the way it ... I always wanted to make a record that you could just put in and push play and not have to skip songs. We feel like we did it. Most people tell us that they can just put it on and let it play, and it spanks the crowd."

I notice a lot of religious imagery with your song titles and a lot of your lyrics and whatnot. What do you think is behind that? What makes you express yourself this way?

DW: "I think when I was a kid, I went through a time in my life where ... I know they were just trying to do the right thing, and be good parents and everything, but there was a period of time where we were going to church quite a bit. We would go from different denominations. We would jump around, like Baptist and Catholic and Methodist and Protestant, pretty much like a buffet. (laughs) We just started to see that, instead of the focus being on, you know, following your heart and about faith, it seemed like the focus was put on a certain man that happened to be speaking that day—that everybody kind of lost sight. So, I think we were sitting in church one day and ... I was sitting between my mom and my dad, and the preacher told us to go home and smash our television, because the devil was sending messages through it. And my father turned to me and said, 'Well, there's a Cowboys game on at noon. I don't think I'm going to smash the TV set today ...' (both laugh) And then I think after that, we just kind of got away from the whole church thing because, like I said, they were putting more emphasis on a person, a preacher, or something, instead of the whole idea. And we stopped going to church. And my dad told me, 'Look, you know, I've always provided for you and your mother ...' People have always told me that, if you swear or if you drink, you're going to hell. And I would analyze that and go, 'Well, my dad has a beer every now and then, and he says a swear word every now and then. Does that mean my father's going to hell?' I just couldn't come to terms with that, so I just put all my faith into music and my family. And those two things have never let me down."

That's interesting ... It sounds like your whole family kind of came to the same decision at the same time.

DW: "Yeah, absolutely."

I grew up in the Dallas area a little. I lived in Richardson.

DW: "Oh wow! I used to live in Plano. You know what I think ... How long has this magazine been around?"

Seventeen years.

DW: "Okay, I think I used to subscribe to it, because when we were going to church and my mom and dad had a big problem with the secular music, like Van Halen and Motley Crue and stuff like that, so I got really into, like, Stryper, Bloodgood, Rez Band, and Barren Cross, and Philadelphia. Like, all the heavy, like, Christian music. I saw Stryper like (expletive) at least fifteen times. Great show. Great music. I remember getting a subscription to this magazine. I was going, 'Aww, this is cool!' I still have Stryper CDs. They're a great band."

We were probably at some of the same shows. I saw 'em at Six Flags in the parking lot there.

DW: "Oh my god! Yeah, I saw that show! That's awesome."

Well, to stay on the subject here, what do you think of Jesus Christ?

DW: "Um, I think He had some good ideas. I think ... It's not so much Him, it's the people that follow Him, ya know? (laughs) There's extremes of anything. My whole thing right now is I'm just kind of believing in—like I said—my music and my family, but I would never knock anybody that goes to church or whatever. And my record is not a, 'Hey, I want you to be this way.' It's more of a telling you, 'Hey, this is how I am' kind of thing. Informative. I personally don't follow, but I have much respect for people. You know, it's all about choice. I would never force my beliefs on anyone, and sometimes that—the Christian beliefs—does get forced on you. Some people can't handle when you tell them you don't necessarily believe in what they believe in. They get a little nervous. I can certainly respect all that. I just personally don't follow."

It doesn't seem to show a lot of thinking when somebody feels threatened by somebody else's belief system.

DW: "Exactly. I've had a lot of people get really upset. I'll have a T-shirt on of a band—a heavy metal band or something like that—and it might be kind of a scary shirt or whatever. I've had people stop me in the mall and go, 'How can you wear that shirt?' And I go, 'Man! It's just a T-shirt. If you're very comfortable in your religion, this T-shirt shouldn't bother you at all.' Not all people are like that. I've got some really good friends that are Christians that don't try to preach to me every day. They understand that this is my life, and I understand that *that* is their life. It's all about choice— personal choice. That's the one thing. Like I said, there's extremes in both. I'm not Marilyn Manson, by any means! I know that's his thing, but I'm a good ole Southern boy that likes his beer and his barbecue and his family and his heavy metal music." (laughs)

One last question about the subject: What do you think about the claims of Jesus to be "the Way, the Truth and the Life; no one comes to the Father but by Me?"

DW: "I've read the Bible from cover to cover, and there is a lot of truth in there. I can see similarities with a lot of things that have gone on and that have come to pass. I think, like I said, it's choice. I don't personally believe that, but if people do … Everybody needs something, you know? If it's Jesus, if it's Satan, if it's alcohol, if it's music, whatever. Everybody needs something. We're very needy people. And we need something to follow, so I completely understand that."

A lot of aggressive music ... sometimes fights will break out ... How do you feel about aggressiveness in music? Some people feel like it's a release, and obviously, some people do release their aggressive energy in a very polite way, just full on getting into the music. How do you feel when fights do break out?

DW: "I absolutely don't like it, of course. I don't advocate violence at all. And we've been very fortunate that we've never had a fight break out at any of our shows. I think that comes down to the artist. I think the vibe that we give off to our fans and our audience is like: 'Look, nobody's here to hurt each other. I want you to go crazy. I want you to have a good time. I want you to get it out of your system, but I don't want you to hurt anybody.' And once they see that vibe coming from us, and us having a good time, I think it kind of puts them at ease, and they do have a good time without getting hurt."

What are your plans for the next two years?

DW: "Let's see ... We're going to do this tour that we're on for six weeks, and then we're going to do Ozzfest Europe and then Ozzfest again in the U.S. After that we'll go back overseas, and then when we come home, we'll take some time off, take a little vacation, and then start working on the second record."

How does it feel to be at this level right now?

DW: "It feels great. I mean, you know, growing up ... I love music so much. I just love going to concerts. I love standing in line for a new Motley Crue record or whatever. It's just been such a big part of my life, and to have it like that and now be on the other side of the complete spectrum of it, it feels good. I always worried that, if it got like this, that I wouldn't be able to handle it, but I've got great parents, I've got great friends, I've got a great band. We all keep each other kind of, 'This is what we always wanted. Let's keep it together.' It's been great. It's all about having a good time, ya know? Just entertainment and music, and it's something that I think's been lost for a couple years—the entertainment value in it—just go out there and playing and having a good time and letting people know that, 'Look, just because

I'm up here and I've sold some records, that doesn't mean I'm any better than you. I'm here to have a good time, just like you are.'"

How would you describe your live show?

DW: "Very intense. Very energetic. We try to make the fans and the audience as much a part of the show as we are. It's visual. It's sonically stimulating. It's just a good ole fashioned Texas (expletive) whoopin'!"

[Originally printed in May/June '02 Issue #95]

"What's a guy named Jesus doing in Jerusalem, know what I'm saying?"

—Wayne Static

16

{ STATIC X

Static X enjoys the privilege of being one of modern metal's prominent bands. A second generation behind Korn and Limp Bizkit, Static X and System of A Down stand out amongst a sea of Ozzfest wannabes. Editor Doug Van Pelt enjoyed getting to chat with "Wayne Static" on his genre, his hair, his fascination with programming, the real Ozzy Osbourne, and his witnessing of the birth and death of nu metal. Here's how the conversation went down ...

Looking back on the last seven to ten years provides an interesting look at musical change. I mean if you take the "X" radio station format as just one example—it's not every day an entire new radio format is born, you know what I mean? As you look back at this broad multi-style genre (that) some people call "X-music" or "nu metal," "aggro," or whatever ... What do you think are significant changes that have happened? Who have been some of the influential artists during this time period, and what excites you, and what disappoints you about this music we are talking about?

WS: "Well, first of all, Korn ... It (nu metal) was peeking maybe a year or two ago when our first album was out. Now it seems that all of the supposedly extreme radio stations are no longer playing extreme music. It only lasted for a couple years. It's been taken over by melodic, less clean versions of extreme music, which is, you know, Staind, Linkin Park, Disturbed—bands like that are really a tamed-down version of the—you know—the whole nu metal thing. I think, in my short career, I have witnessed sort of the rise and fall of nu metal—the way I see it."

If you saw the music you were making being packaged and sold in way that made you feel marginalized or superficial, what sort of efforts and attitudes would you take to steer your art out of this box?

WS: "You can only steer your art so much. Static X is Static X. We will always be the members of the band. I think you lean one direction or the other direction—as we did on our second record. We leaned a little more in the heavier direction. But you still have to be sure of what you are and sure of what makes your band popular. I think you have to be sure not to change too much (from) album to album over your career ..."

What is the most brutal or grotesque act of violence you have seen in the live audience or onstage?

WS: "Well, the worst things I've seen was the security guys beating up kids that were crowd surfing early on—before we really had good security. When things first started taking off for us, there were two shows that the crowd was maybe a little more than the promoters expected. They didn't have enough security guys there. I followed them taking the kids out of the crowd and out back and beat on them and stuff, but that was the last time that happened. From there on out, we always had security meet our people before the show to explain exactly what we expect of them."

That's pretty cool that you do that. That security problem happens way too much.

WS: "Yeah, we've reached a level that we have better security now than we used to, or maybe they're learning that we gotta tolerate the crowd surfing. It's not an evil thing. You've got to deal with it in its proper context."

Have you seen the movie *We Sold Our Soul For Rock And Roll* by Penelope Spheeris?

WS: "I never got to see it."

I was going to ask you how you thought that compared with the up-close scenes with Ozzy as compared to the current *Osbournes* show on MTV. It showed him taking hits of oxygen and doing all kinds of vitamins to make it through a show ...

WS: "I spent a little time with Ozzy here and there. We did do two Ozzfests. To me, the show makes him out to be a little more of a senile, helpless old man than he really is. I think the show is really poking fun at him, which is fun if you like that. I don't think he's as helpless and senile as the show makes him out to be. My experience has been that he is very quick-witted and very aware of what is going on. It just so happens—between his accent and the way he mumbles—it is hard to understand what it is he is saying sometimes. So, I don't think the show is completely accurate."

How involved were you with the Chaos Comics project, and how fulfilling was that?

WS: "The band has been very involved with that. We had discussions about story line ideas, styles of artwork we wanted to use ... We've been involved every step of the way. I think it's a really cool thing. Not many bands have comic books released."

Yeah, no kidding. What do you think of Jesus Christ?

WS: "Um, boy, *that's* a really good question. I don't know if I want to get into all of that. There's going to be a lot of people that have different opinions. People are very passionate about their religious beliefs. I'd rather not get involved in an argument."

What do you think about a kind of friendly, public debate of a question or two?

WS: "What do I think about a public debate about Jesus Christ?"

Yeah.

WS: "I don't think it's possible, because people believe absolutely in their own religious beliefs, and there is no way ... it would become an argument. There is no way to have a debate about it. Everyone is so passionate in their beliefs—they believe completely that they are right—and I don't think it's possible. There's very few people who have an open mind about these things ..."

Right. I've seen very some good conversations take place when people do try to approach it with more of an open mind and the two showing the other person dignity no matter what—letting the other person speak and hold their position.

(Pauses for comment and then moves to next question.) Much of the sci-fi movies and books about the future world seem less outlandish now in the wake of terrorism on our soil, in my opinion. What role do you think technology plays in society in either a positive light or a negative one?

WS: "I think technology is not going to be developing as much as it did in the last twenty years. I think we're at a leveling off point. Things are so expensive now, and there are so many other problems. For instance, the space program's never going to advance any further than it is right now 'cause there is nothing to fuel it. There's no Cold War. Computers—I don't see how they can become much more a part of everyone's life than they already are. To me, I am not a fan of the Internet, really. I think it's just really a huge invasion of my privacy, and my music gets stolen every day on the Internet. People can say anything they want about any celebrity they want, and people might take it as the truth. I don't know ... to me, I am not a fan of that. I think the world would be fine without it. If they read the newspapers and watched the news on TV, they could get all the info they needed, or if they went to the library (and) looked it up in a book. It was a tiny bit more effort for everyone, but I think everyone had a lot more privacy."

Yeah, I think it certainly breeds reactionary behavior, like with message boards and email and chat rooms—people just say what they think without really thinking about it, and then, boom, hit the send button.

WS: "Yeah, there's something about seeing words in print—they have so much more of an effect than someone just saying something, you know?"

True. You guys recently covered Elvis and the Ramones on a couple of different compilations. How have either of these artists influenced you, and how do you enjoy or not enjoy covering their songs?

WS: "The Ramones song was a lot of fun. It was easy. We were all fans of the Ramones, so to me, that was a lot of fun—to do something different, and, punk being fun, it wasn't a huge stretch for us. We just tried to make the song our own, which is what we always do when we do cover songs. The Elvis song was a bit of a stretch. It was some work to pull that one off, and I am not even sure if I like it after everything we did to it. I know it's cool and everything, but it's such a different animal for us, but Elvis is my mom's favorite, so she still has an Elvis poster hanging up in her and my dad's bedroom. That was a big deal for her, but I grew up listening to Elvis all of the time. I am a fan of Elvis. It's just a very different style of music than what I would normally do."

You moved from Chicago to L.A. a while back. How would you compare and contrast the two cities? Do you miss Chicago?

WS: "I've never missed Chicago for a second. There's a lot of reasons. I moved to Chicago when I was very young. I was heavy into partying there. I did a lot of growing up there, and I think I burned a lot of bridges there. I feel like I used that town up. It used me up. When it was time to go, it was time to go. I didn't even tell anyone I was leaving; I just left. So, I probably have a very sort of jaded attitude about Chicago. It is just a very conservative city. It's a huge city with lots of very conservative people from the Midwest that moved there, where L.A. is this whole sprawling animal of different cultures and different ideas. Everything is tolerated so much more here, or maybe it's just the weather—it keeps people in a better mood ... I don't know, but L.A. is more of a home than Chicago ever was."

That's interesting. I live in Austin, Texas, and it's definitely like a liberal hotbed in a very conservative state. I recently read a fascinating novel based on the premise of Jesus coming to earth for the first time in Chicago in the year 2000. It was a lot of fun to read, because I've been to Chicago, and there were a lot of accurate details regarding street names, landmarks, and neighboring suburbs.

Can you give us a primer on who you would consider the seminal industrial metal artists of our time?

WS: "Well, it's gotta be Ministry. I started listening to industrial music probably around '82 or '83, and that was around the time when Ministry was starting, and they kinda led the whole movement, which was born in Chicago with Wax Trax records. Ministry was the first band that really broke out of the original mold of mixing the hip-hop type of industrial music, and they made it dark and brought it hard and really shook it up. I don't think anyone would disagree with me that they were at the forefront of the whole thing. They opened up a whole new way of thinking for a band like ourselves, for bands like Rob Zombie, Prong, which is not around right now, and lots of other industrial bands that followed as well."

Cool. It's a great style of music. You've toured with some very cool bands over the years. What are some of your favorite memories?

WS: "Probably one of the really cool things was during the Family Values Tour late last year. It was my birthday on the tour, and very unexpectedly, halfway through our show, every band member from the whole tour came onstage and brought me cake and gag gifts and stuff. That was pretty cool, because it was a lot of people that I really respect (who) were on that tour. It was great bands. That was a real nice memory. And, on a different type of thing, we were in Mexico with Korn recently, and we did a show in Mexico City. It was the biggest show we've ever played. It was 55,000 people in a soccer stadium. That was probably the most fun I've ever had, actually, performing. It wasn't like (only) half the people were into it. They were on their seats, jumping around, screaming all the way back to the stands. It was an incredible, magical experience."

That sounds rad. How did you recently get involved in programming and sampling? And what led you to experiment with that realm, and what do you credit for any leaps you have made in your progress—both technically and artistically?

WS: "Well, up until about '95, I had never really had any sampling or programming elements in our music. I had always been a fan of it, but I never owned a board or anything like that. So, around that time, shortly after Ken (Jay, drummer) and I moved out here in L.A., trying to start the band all over, we were experimenting with all kinds of styles, trying to figure out what we wanted to do with this band, and one night I was listening to a couple of my old Ministry records, and some of the early stuff—the *Twitch* album in particular—doesn't even have any guitar on it. And I had this idea of, 'What if we make this our main single and start making things a little rigid in terms of more drum machine style and sort of use the guitars more like keyboards than the traditional guitars?'

"That was kind of where it all started. I had this crappy, ten-year-old Alesis drum machine laying around, and I pulled that out and started messing around with it. We developed our style that way, and I instantly felt the magic. Then we started working that direction and stayed with it.

"Originally, I didn't even know what a sampler was until our first record. All the samples were just thrown in manually off of cassette tapes. I think that is how our style of programming developed. Now it's so much different than a lot of the other bands. Now I actually have the money to buy samplers. I think that is why, in a way, we sound like we do. It added such a low-tech kind of a vibe to everything we do. It had to be created with the crappy equipment that we had."

That's cool. Maybe that gave it more of an organic feel. Well, how has your vertical hairstyle changed your life? Describe some experiences that some of us with less outlandish hairstyles could never identify with.

WS: "Well, sort of the hairstyle and myself have become one. We've kind of grown together as my career has progressed. My whole stage persona has kind of melded with my hairstyle and become one, but having said that, I really don't like wearing my hair that way out on the street, because I am at a point now in my life where I'm trying to blend in and not stand out and create attention—like I tried to do when I was eighteen years old. Now I don't want to be recognized on the street. But I remember one time in particular when I first met my current girlfriend and I went to church one Sunday, maybe it was Easter or something, and I had my hair up, which was probably a mistake, but I remember walking down an aisle and this woman holding a baby in her arms in a predominantly Hispanic congregation, and the baby looked at me and started crying and screaming, 'Diablo! Diablo!' (laughs) So, that was the last time I wore my hair up at church for sure."

Wisconsin Death Trip has now gone platinum. Do feel like the longer road to platinum status, as opposed to the quick trip, is more rewarding—both mentally and fiscally? Why or why not?

WS: "I don't think anyone would argue that a slow, steady rise can build a more loyal fan base than a one-hit wonder overnight kind of deal. No one is going to argue that. But, having said that, I think maybe the slow rise kinda takes away from the high you might get from getting such an honor. When our album went platinum, I was like, 'Oh yeah, that's cool. What are we going to have for dinner?' It was like so long to get there, that by the time it was there, it was like … I saw it coming months before that, so I was already mentally prepared. I think it was more of a shock for us was when our second record came out and sold, like 83,000 in the first week. To me, that was way more of a shock than our first album going platinum."

Gotcha. Well, how does a band in your position replace a guitarist?

WS: "Uh, very carefully. When Fukuda left, we were like, "Well, geez. What are we going to do now?" I knew that we could record the album without him. It was more, 'What are we going to do live? How are we going to find a guitar player that can stand up onstage in front of 20,000 people every night?' It's scary. There was only one guy that I knew that was a good enough player and a great showman, and I knew he could handle it, and that was Tripp (Rex Eisen). As fate would have it, Tripp was leaving a situation at the same time that Fukuda left Static X. He actually called me, 'Hey, I heard you need a guitar player,' and it seemed to work out. It was really an awesome thing. I really feel bad for somebody like Limp Bizkit, who, you know, they lost Wes. I talked with those guys last week, and they still haven't found one. They're still auditioning two people a day, five days a week. They haven't found one they're happy with, so that's really tough for them."

Wow. Well, tell me about *Machine*. What do you like about it, and what sort of lyrical themes do you hope your listeners will dig into and discover or get?

WS: "I feel like it's a more cohesive album than our first album. Personally, I think it's a better album. Maybe it's just because I felt more comfortable with our style. I felt we had developed our musical style at that point, and we are just trying to write great, killer songs; where, on the first album, we were still experimenting a lot with which direction we wanted to hit. It was a lot of fun recording it. We thought, 'Hey, let's just go ahead and make this record a little heavier and not be afraid to just have fun with it.'

"We didn't really hold back at all. We went balls out. Lyrically, I think it's a very personal record. You know, it's a lot of road stories and feelings that goes with being on the road, questioning whether that's what you wanna do with your life, feelings you (have about) maybe your girlfriend that you haven't seen in two months—all kinds of stuff like that."

Cool. I'll take one more stab at this. What do you think of the following quote: "I am the Way, the Truth and the Life; no comes to Father but by Me?"

WS: "What do I think about that? (laughs) Why do you, like, bend on all this stuff? Are you trying to convert me here or something?"

Well, I'm just trying to engage a dialogue that's very intriguing to a lot of people.

WS: "Yeah."

You know, spiritual discussions...

WS: "I think the Bible is a great story. I think it has been over-analyzed. I think that there may be a lot of truth in there. I feel like there's a lot embellishment in the text that may have occurred in the past. It's a great book, and it helps a lot of people through really hard times. Do I believe in it 100 percent? I don't know. There's a lot of problems, I think ... What's a guy named Jesus doing in Jerusalem, know what I'm saying?"

Yeah.

WS: "There's just so many problems there. (laughs) It doesn't make any sense, you know. But I see the value of it, so I would never criticize anyone who really takes it to heart and it helps them be a better person in their life."

Well, I hope the interview wasn't too weird. I was using this mute button on my phone. I got a really low signal on this end. It's like a real low impedance or something, so you're missing all the uh-huhs, yeahs, cools, and wows and laughter that I might interject ... when you're having a conversation with somebody. So, I hope it wasn't too weird.

WS: "Interesting questions. No, I think I've been asked about everything. I've only been asked about Christ one other time, and I got in trouble when I answered it truthfully last time. So, hopefully I won't get in trouble this time."

[Originally printed in July/August '02 Issue #96]

"I believe
Christ is the way
to heaven and
through Him,
prayer is
heard by God."

—Eliot Sloan

17

BLESSID UNION
OF SOULS

photo by Larry Busacca

Blessid Union of Souls, a pop/rock band known for number one songs like "I Believe," "Let Me Be The One," and "Light in Your Eyes," started as a songwriting team that debuted with the album Home *in 1995. Six years and four albums later, HM interviewer Ginny McCabe sat down with the band (Eliot Sloan, Jeff Pence, C.P. Roth, Eddie Hedges, and Tony Clark) for a conversation about their religious backgrounds, the measure of success, Ozzy Osbourne, and making music for a living.*

How would you describe the hard rock music culture today? How do you think it compares to ten or twenty years ago?

JP: "I think it connects with a lot more people, naturally. Ninety-five percent of hard rock in the '90s seemed to be about pain and suffering. I don't think 95 percent of the people listening to rock really feel like that every day. I know we all do sometimes, but I really like what I hear on harder rock radio stations today."

CR: "Well, like everything else, no ugly guys are allowed to be rock stars anymore, and even the ugly ones are basically metal acts in Kabuli makeup. Hey, it worked for Paul and Gene! (There are) a few bright points. Incubus really has their finger on treading the line between pop success, metal cred, and is still innovative with the way they write and record. Also, Tool, my faves of the genre, is about the closest thing to the progressive bands of the '70s that I can remember, yet they sound totally current and fresh. Keep in mind that MTV's and boy pop's legacy to the way the music biz is going to break new acts has not been lost on the alt metal scene. One need only look at cookie cutter bands like Sum 41, traceable back to Green Day ... traceable back to the Buzzcocks ... who were ugly, to see that visual marketing is being very carefully considered here. I can only imagine a guy like Springsteen trying to start out now. I've been listening to hard rock/metal since the Music Machine recorded "Talk Talk" in 1966. One nice thing about this music is that it really does require some sort of virtuosity to perform correctly, so even if they all end up looking like Jim Henson's Satan Babies, some good music will still emerge from this."

Do you see any major musical trends happening right now?

JP: "I think bands are coming back, and singing boy bands are going away."

EH: "We have played everywhere. We are one of those bands that have actually hit the road, and we've done a lot of it. Hootie and the Blowfish did that, and Dave Matthews Band are examples of other bands, real bands, who have gotten out there and played. The problem is that you have so many groups that have records out, who really are not even a band. Either they are out doing tracks dates, singing to a tape, or a sequencer, or some kind of canned music. That gets old after a while ... If you want to hear a band, and be entertained by a band, there are a few of us out there. We survive because we give people a good show, and we sound like we do on the record, and it isn't prerecorded music, and of course, the songs."

CR: "R&B has gotten good again, and it's about time. This has been a long time in coming, but now there a number of new artists that finally seem to get it. I see this movement starting with artists like Erykah Badu and Macy Gray, to say nothing of the groundbreaking work that Missy Elliott has done with Timbaland.

"But now, due to the commercial success of this sound, labels are finding similar artists who all have their own unique take on things that include Blu Cantrell, Jill Scott, and Nikka Costa. The basis of this sound, to my ears anyway, seems rooted in the early '70s records of Stevie Wonder, Marvin Gaye, as well as a number of female artists of the day who never got their due, including Syreeta Wright, Millie Jackson, and the most extreme diva ever, Betty Davis, an ex-wife of Miles Davis, who made records so funky, they made the Ohio Players sound like the Indigo Girls. For this old rocker, I am in heaven."

Why do you think Blessid Union's music is relevant to listeners, today?

TC: "We bring our life experiences into what we write about. And, everybody in the band comes from a different background, completely—both socially and musically. I think for some reason, that makes us gel really well."

ES: "(Our songs are about) life and everything around. I have written songs that don't really apply to me. I may have gotten them from a movie, or an idea from a movie, but they really don't apply to my life specifically. I just write as things come to me. Sometimes I may even get an idea for a song out of the blue."

The band has a lot of combined musical experience, even prior to the formation of Blessid Union of Souls. C.P., you previously toured with Ozzy Osbourne. What was that experience like?

CR: "Well, the thing I tell folks about this, Blessid Union, versus that, my gig with Ozzy, is with Oz, I was being paid a lot of money to convince myself

I was a rock star, and with the Blessids, we pay a lot of other people a lot of money to convince us that we're rock stars! Touring with Ozzy was magic. Everything was five-star. And, he was really funny and very generous. Plus, it was totally cool to be in a touring band of Oz's that included Geezer Butler from Sabbath ... This was during the absolute peak of hair metal, 1988-89. (Who knew) in two short years, some kid from Seattle named Kurt was going to change everything?"

How well did you get to know Ozzy, and how would you describe him as a person?

CR: "I would imagine I got to know him as well as most folks who work with him. But, I don't think in the bigger picture that's very close at all. He is a huge Beatles fanatic, and believe me, I know some Beatles fanatics in New York City that need de-programming, but Oz is just nuts for them. He'd come in the dressing room, and Zack (Wylde) would be jamming some Priest or Guns on the blaster, and Oz would just hit stop and throw in *Sgt. Pepper's Lonely Hearts Club Band* or *The White Album* and just stare into space listening to it. He's also an all-time pro practical joker; you have to watch yourself around this guy."

Did you get any kind of feel for what his religious beliefs were?

CR: "I think it was pretty much Church Of England, tempered by some real world philosophy he picked up as a young street fighter in Birmingham, U.K. Look, that Satan thing? All an act. Most of the time, he does stuff just to piss off the holy rollers who are using him to sell their brand of snake oil, and it is amazing the stuff he has to deal with just by being 'Ozzy.' You have no idea."

What about the way some people feel he portrays himself onstage?

CR: "Well, again, the tour I did had this very strange thing happen. We were to play a gig in Portland, Oregon, and stay there, but at the last minute, everything got switched, and we stayed in Seattle because some nutso five and dime preacher had threatened to picket the gig and the hotel with 2,500 supporters to rid the town of evil. What we found out this guy had been selling his 'flock,' was that at our show in San Diego (three weeks prior), Ozzy had reportedly taken—I am SO NOT making this up—'a box of puppies and threw them into the crowd and told them that unless they ripped the dogs apart, that he would not play another note'?!

"Not only did this not ever happen—no dogs, no nothing—anywhere, but Oz is a total animal lover. He absolutely freaks out when he sees anyone or thing getting hurt at his shows. Anyway, that night security was very tight, and everyone was on edge that there was gonna be some sorta confrontation at the gig—that is until this idiot showed up with twenty 'supporters' who were kind of ignored by the kids coming into the venue ... Ozzy has to constantly deal with these fifth-rate vultures who simultaneously use him as a living icon for everything bad, while sponging off his celebrity (status) to enhance theirs. Swell ..."

Comparing your experience with Ozzy Osbourne and his harder style of music to the rock/pop stylings of Blessid Union of Souls, there seems to be some major differences style-wise. What style do you prefer? Why didn't you stick with the harder rock style?

CR: "Look, I have never been a purist. It has always seemed to me that purists were just guys who got tired of moving forward. And, if you look at this band's musical output, pure is about the furthest thing from what we do. There are six distinctly different guys in this band, including Emosia/ 3XL, our co-songwriter and co-producer, with six totally different takes on music and its different processes. If I was doing a solo thing, it would be much more electronic in nature, but our job is to make this the best version of Blessid Union there is. That makes it more of a challenge to everyone, and that's a good thing. You get the best of everyone's contributions that way."

Can you talk a little about your "punk rock" days, prior to your experience with Ozzy, and how that prepared you for what you are doing now?

CR: "Like most other things, it was all a happy accident. I had just completed my music school studies at Manhattan School of Music, and I was ready for something. That something was the burgeoning punk scene happening downtown in New York City (in 1977). I started checking it out and really liked what I saw and heard. There was a lot of innovative stuff that never saw the light of day on any level outside the 'scene' itself. There was a great deal of creative freedom that was appreciated by the people coming to see this stuff. This gave me the chance to try some very, very dodgy things out onstage just to see if they could be pulled off. That was a huge thing, because I was working with about eight bands at once, doing everything from pure punk, to neo-girl group stuff, to early electronica, plus doing dance records and jingle dates during the day. Many of the people I knew and worked with became huge stars coming out of that scene. It was a very rosy time, and I am blessed to have been a small part of it.

"I had my first record contract deal as a result of all of this, signing with a band called Regina Richards and Red Hot. We were discovered by the same guy who discovered Blondie. We did one album, which only got released by A&M Records in the U.K. However, I did learn a lot about the record business, and it was mostly bad. It did prepare me for a lot of the stuff we have went through, and are still going through to one extent or another ..."

What about other early musical influences?

ES: "I really got into Led Zeppelin. I don't even know what it was; I really got drawn into them. I couldn't understand a word Robert Plant was saying, but it sounded good, and it felt good. There was a real magic to that. I love Queen. I love Prince, and I was so into Prince. Prince was the reason that I wanted to do this ... He came out with the *1999* album, and that helped seal the deal. And, I've bought that record three or four times since then."

TC: "I learned a lot taking the theory courses in school. I grew up learning how to read music, but not really exploring the other side of it, by applying that kind of training to today's pop/rock music. It was playing live shows that gave me more of an opportunity to begin to apply what I learned in music theory classes to the world of today's rock music."

EH: "Everybody in my family started out in music. Our Dad and Mom took us to church, so we were involved. My brother Billy and I have pursued music as a career."

This interview is for *HM*, a Christian magazine that covers hard music. I wanted to talk to you a little bit about your beliefs. What did they believe in "religiously," and how did they bring you up in that regard?

CR: "Mom is as WASP as they come, having been raised in Yellow Springs, Ohio. Pop is a second generation Jewish kid, whose family hails from Odessa, Russia. They both gave me a somewhat small window at a very early age to take in certain things about both their faiths, but I didn't really get it. Over time, I have adopted most of my dad's Jewish philosophy, tempered by a lot of Dickens, which he read to me and my brother constantly, along with the Old Testament, and Tarzan, when we were young. What can I say? I'm old school."

ES: "My grandmother (Nora, from the *Home* CD) was the one who really instilled a sense of church and belief in me when I was a child, basically to keep me out of trouble."

You should get a copy of the New Testament—The Message. The Old Testament is focused more on law. The New Testament is about life, and abundant life through Jesus Christ. What do you think of Jesus Christ?

CR: "I think He needs new representation! ... I do not want to seem trite over this ... Eliot and Eddie are both strong Christians."

ES: "(I think) He is the Savior, the Way, the Truth, and the Life."

What do you think of His claims to be "the Way, the Truth, and the Life; no one comes to the Father but by Me?"

CR: "Me? I'm still wondering how Moses got that bush to burn."

ES: "I pretty much summed it up with my previous answer. I believe the Bible and Jesus so much, that it's hard to fathom believing anything else, but everyone has their own reasons for believing what they believe."

I think Jesus is who He says He is, and His claims are true. I think a key factor is not so much about religion, but having a daily one-on-one relationship with Jesus Christ. I believe it's important to read the Bible, live out its principles in your life, and really get to know Jesus in a personal way. Though we are all human beings and fail, God's grace and mercy help to bring us into a right and perfect relationship with Him. How would you describe your religious beliefs today?

ES: "I believe Christ is the way to heaven and through Him, prayer is heard by God."

How would you explain what you believe in to someone else?

ES: "I believe the Bible is God's Word."

What kind of statement do you think your music makes?

JP: "We don't try to make any statements; at least I don't. I just want to rock and have fun."

What advice would you give to other musicians? Why?

JP: "Remember, if you want to be in the music business, you're playing or writing music for other people to enjoy and, hopefully, buy. If you play or write music for yourself, then it's a hobby, and have fun with it."

Jeff, what do you think makes you stand out as a musician?

JP: "I don't think I stand out as a musician, but more as a motivator."

What about the name of the band, can you explain that to me?

EH: "Like with anything, the nice guy image has good and bad connotations. A lot of times, because you are a nice guy, a lot of people don't perceive you as a cool guy. This music industry itself is kind of wacky, in that sometimes, your image takes precedence over your sound and what you do, what you play, and the music that you do. It is sad, but true.

"Even with the name Blessid Union of Souls, when we came out in the beginning, a lot of people thought we were a Christian band, not that there's anything wrong with that, because there are Christians in the band; it is just that it's a turn-off sometimes to radio, and definitely music television. It's sad because a lot of people look at that, and they turn away from that; they think, 'Oh, they're a Christian group, they don't want to rock.' It has (sometimes) been a turn off, just the name itself. It doesn't really matter to us, because we do what we do."

ES: "I originally came up with the name of the band from a line I heard in a *M.A.S.H.* episode. I wanted to use the unusual spelling because I wanted people to pronounce it BLESS-ID."

Musically, what is ahead for Blessid Union?

EH: "Once again, we have all been gifted to play our instruments, and we know how to (present) a good show—not to say a lot of other bands can't do that, but there are a lot of entertainers out there, and the whole band thing is almost a lost art. Over the last year, or two years, it has been the era of the boy band, pre-recorded music type of thing. I think we have survived because we go out there and do a good show. People walk away saying, 'Those guys rock.'"

TC: "I look at it, and I think it is really (cool) that we have had that many singles that we can put out this kind of album, like *The Singles*. It says a lot in the fact that we've put out that many hits over five years that we can contribute them to a first volume of singles like this. And, in a few more years, I hope we have just as many hit songs, so that we can put them on a second volume."

CR: "... You have to constantly come up with the goods. Some bands will have a career based on one song that they can stretch out for a number of years, because that song has a particular type of success. We want (to) provide listeners with songs they want to hear ... When it comes to the end of the day, we have to sit down and write good music."

[Originally printed in May/June '02 Issue 95]

"I'm down with
J.C. He's cool.
Whatever."

—Mike Dirnt

If you have been even the least bit aware of the worldwide music scene in the last two years of this past millennium, you've heard of Green Day. Their Dookie *album made it into millions of hands. They played Woodstock. They've been on the cover of* Rolling Stone. *When a band gets this big and this important, it's time for HM magazine to put on its spiritual sleuth hat and find out what these guys think of the Creator of all things—Jesus Christ. In this phone interview, HM editor Doug Van Pelt tries to get bassist Mike Dirnt to explain how he feels about the person of Jesus.*

Where do you see both yourself and Green Day in five years?

MD: "I don't look that far ahead. None of us do. It's like, we don't look too far into the future. Here today, gone later today, you know? We're very happy with what we've done so far, and if we can continue to put out music that makes us happy—and we're happy with it, then I'm sure there will be a good amount of people who will like it. That would be a great place to be in five years—still playing our music and enjoying playing."

Definitely. What's your favorite childhood memory?

MD: "Hmm, my favorite childhood memory ... I used to ride my bicycle a lot. I was silly on bicycles when I was a little kid, like, from the age of two, it seemed like. I got a lot of good little ones (memories) from when I was a little kid. But, I don't know. I guess none of that really matters right now."

How do you like or dislike the touring musician lifestyle?

MD: "I don't think we have the typical touring musician lifestyle. Well, we work a hard shift—we hit the road every night. We don't stay in hotels. But, we have the most exciting job on tour, because we get to play one hour a day. We live for that, but we also have the most boring job on tour, you know, doing interviews and standing around all day—hurrying up and waiting. So it's a hard one for sure. I miss my fiancé like crazy. She's not always with me on tour, because it's even more boring for her."

Where are you at today?

MD: "Today we're in Chicago."

Do you believe in evolution? Why or why not?

MD: "Yes I do, because I watched it happen for four records. Because I feel that *Insomniac* evolved perfectly after *Dookie*. Evolution of people, yeah. I believe in evolution of people. So, yeah man. You know, when Beck said, 'In a time of chimpanzees, I was a monkey,' well I was also a monkey. I'm sure of it. I just feel it in my bones."

Is that what you base your belief on?

MD: "You know what? I'm an optimistic agnostic. I think the second we die, within a matter of seconds, everybody else arrives, and that's the party, and you live your hell on earth. I don't know."

What do you think of Jesus Christ?

MD: "I'm down with J.C. He's cool. Whatever."

What do you think of His claims to be the Way, the Truth, and the Life, "No one comes to the Father but by Me?"

MD: "Sounds a little mafioso to me. You know, to each their own. Everyone has the right to believe in whatever they believe in. Like I said, I'm an optimist, so I believe in some sort of life after death, I don't know what kind."

Have you ever thought about how there's this guy here, everybody says He was a great teacher and all. He went around saying He's the only Way to the Father, and then He died for that statement.

MD: "I'm sure that He did. I'm sure that a lot of people have died for that, but I'm sure more people have died arguing over it since then. You know, millions. And when I hear people say that everybody in the world has heard of Jesus Christ, it makes me want to puke, in all honesty. I'm not gonna base my religion, well, I base my religion on my own spirituality, and 'what goes around comes around.' If there is a God or anything like that, there's nothing I can certainly do about it. I believe we're all part of the force. It's like the force. There's Luke, there's Laia, and there's us."

Us meaning me and you, or Green Day?

MD: "As in the world."

Well, everybody bases their beliefs on something ...

MD: "All my religious beliefs are based on *Star Wars*."

I bet you're pretty excited about the trilogy coming out.

MD: "You better believe it. I am totally excited."

How did the success feel to you?

MD: "It's nice to know that people can get our music, and that people relate to it, and that we can go all over the world and the people that we play to can buy our records now. The exciting part to me is when you go somewhere that you've never been before, or you go somewhere that you *have* been before, and you feel the connection. There's a camaraderie. Everyone's there for the music. I think it's great. I don't stop and look back and lay on my laurels at all. We're all too busy thinking about what's going on in the future. Not the far future, though, mainly today till tonight."

How do you respond to the critics who say, "Green Day isn't punk"?

MD: "I agree. (laughs) It's kind of an oxymoron to say 'punk rock' and 'hockey arena' at the same time. We definitely come from a certain element, and we have a certain idea of what we like. We carry our morals, our ideals, our ethics, everything with us from where we come from. But I can't say I am the same person as who I was five years ago. I'd be kidding myself. I think that's the most important thing you can do to be a real person—is to be honest with yourself."

Do you get people that get kind of down on you now that you're not underground anymore?

MD: "Not at all. Well, I can't say not at all. I'm sure there are, but it's not a problem. I mean, we make music for people who want to hear our music, and we make music for ourselves. Call us greedy, call us selfish. We make music for ourselves. When we create these CDs, we give 'em to people, and it's theirs to pick and poke and prod at, or to love and to hold and to cherish, or whatever you want to do with it. I think that's all really important, because for me, and I think for most musicians, even if they don't know it, but part of the greatest joy of playing music at all is sharing music and playing it for people."

Are you a speed freak?

MD: "Am I a what?"

A speed freak.

MD: "No, but we have a lot of friends who are. Northern California is kind of one of the meth-amphetamine capitals of the world. Let's just say we have a lot of friends who've gone that direction. I've dabbled here and there. We all have, but we are not speed freaks. We are insomniacs, but we're not speed freaks. There's a generational thing with a lot of the lyrics on this album. Like 'Geek Stink Breath,' a lot of people twenty or thirty years ago, people don't know what speed is. And they don't know that people who do speed lose their teeth constantly and pick scabs off their face constantly, and it eats holes in their brains, and whatever. But that's really a prevalent thing, where we come from."

What do you think of the band MxPx?

MD: "MxPx?"

Yeah, they're called Magnified Plaid. They go by MxPx.

MD: "I have no idea who they are. I'm sure they're great. I'm sure they're the greatest thing ever. I don't know. I'm really open-minded in that aspect."

Judging from my reading of the lyrics to the infectious song, "Eighty-Six," I get the impression that you hate corporate heavy metal. How do you feel about it?

MD: "The song's more about not being able to go and hang out in your old stomping ground. It's just how Billy felt for a matter of time, you know, and put it in perspective. It's like a friend stopped by his house, a friend he hadn't seen in a long time. Said, 'What brings you around? Did you lose something last time you were here?' And you know, just kind of coming to terms with the fact that you can't go back to the years of whenever, or you can't go back to yesterday."

I just took my best shot at it.

MD: "That song's got a neat position, because it's jaded. There's kind of like a resolution to that, and that is: 'Don't be jaded and think that the only best times of your life are already over.'"

That's what I think about suicide. You have no idea what's gonna happen five years down the road.

MD: "That's the thing. Songs are just expressions of emotions at times, or how you feel about a particular subject at times. Me personally, I can't swing really far to the right for a long time. I can't be like totally pissed off for days or years, unless I had a dramatic change in my life or something. But chances are, given time, most wounds will heal—most. And of course this is earth and we are mortal ... emotionally speaking, I guess."

How do you attempt to keep your feet on the ground now that you're kind of riding this crest of popularity?

MD: "Just don't put yourself on a pedestal and think it's more than it is, because you're here today and gone later today. We don't go out and buy Ferraris and throw the rock 'n' roll lifestyle—not at all. I'm surprised the question isn't, 'How can you afford such an exceedingly poor punk lifestyle?' Well, I'll tell you how I do it. I give all my money to my mom. Everybody who buys a record, I send 'em a dollar. (laughs) I don't know. We've been weaned into it really well. We'd been going on tour years before we ever got to a major label. So we'll go on tour for months, and we'll come back, and our friends'll give us a head check. And that's been happening for, you know ... we'll leave for two months, come back, leave for three months, come back, and every time, our friends give us a head check. I think that we're pretty firmly grounded in who we are and where we come from. As to where we want to go, well, see ya when we get there."

Well, heading back for the last question, about *Star Wars* and the force, what would be your best idea about what kind of force is out there, what kind of supreme being or spiritual world awaits us?

MD: "That's a strange thing, because life is so amazing that people will argue. They will argue this and that, or whatever. I think that everything is connected in one way or another. I bet I'm connected to some star that is hundreds and hundreds, and zillions of miles away. If there is a God, it's something I can't even fathom. So, why spend my life trying to understand something that I can't understand? I just take my morals and my scruples out of whatever I have learned in life and just go with that. I don't know. It's got to be something like a force."

What if there was a God? Could you see, like, how someone could be a fanatic, and there really was a God, and you could know of Him?

MD: "I had an ex-girlfriend who left me for Jesus. I thought I was gonna marry this girl, a long time ago."

How did that go?

MD: "It didn't. She went to Los Angeles to a Christian Bible college, and did her thing, which is fine. That's great, you know? I don't so much find myself bitter. I just think that she was jaded in a lot of respects. She wanted to become a psychiatrist, only it goes against her church, so in total tears and agony, she's now decided she can't do that. And that's pretty upsetting considering she could've been a pretty good psychologist. Maybe she could've worked out some of her own problems. I think she's wishing the best. I think that religion has a lot to do with family. I don't think that pumping fear into people is a good way to get them to have morals. Pumping love into people is a better way, and I'm not a hippie."

I just interviewed Geezer Butler today, and I mentioned to him how they came out with Black Sabbath in the days of hippie music, and here they came out with music that blew the wallpaper off walls and stomped on hippies' heads.

MD: "I wouldn't go stomp on anyone's head either, though. I do unto others as I would like to have done unto me. I'm a pretty mellow person, I think."

Well, they aren't really like that, either. I don't want to portray them as that.

But I agree with you in that fear is not a very good motivator.

MD: "It's just that when I was a little kid, I had a pastor tell me ... you know, I was really confused by a few of the sermons I'd heard, and I asked him, I said, 'My mother smokes cigarettes. Will she go to hell if she smokes cigarettes?' And he said, 'Yes.' And I was seven years old. That was (expletive). I was at church with a friend of mine's family, and it was really (expletive). So I go home thinking my mom's gonna burn in eternal hell, in eternal damnation. In my opinion, heaven is not a place where all my friends aren't. You live your hell on earth, and there might be something further to it than that, but afterwards, our spirit kind of takes off. That's why I'm gonna be cremated. I don't want to be stuck in any box. Maybe they'll bury me upside down and plant a seed in my (expletive).

[Originally printed in April/May '96 Issue #58]

"He certainly walked the earth. I do not believe some of the claims people have about Him."

—Ian Anderson

JETHRO TULL

photo by Martyn Goddard

This issue our "What So & So Says" feature brings us to Ian Anderson of the classic rock staple Jethro Tull. Listen in as Ian and HM Editor Doug Van Pelt discuss music and faith.

How has the audience response to progressive music such as yours changed over the last three and a half decades?

IA: "There are people who love this kind of music ... We've enjoyed a very positive response over the years. It's amazing to see young new faces coming to our shows, but we primarily have an older audience."

How much do you consider the age of your audience when writing a song?

IA: "Not at all. First and foremost, I write for myself. I started out as a visual artist. I painted. I gravitated towards music because of the drama of live performance. I make music for myself, and for the band, and the audience, I'm afraid, comes last."

What have been some of the more interesting concert billings you have experienced with Jethro Tull?

IA: "In '69 we were the support act for Led Zeppelin. That was very good, and we learned a lot from Led Zeppelin about performing. A few months later we began headlining ourselves. We toured with Jimi Hendrix between '69 and '71. We saw some amazing performances ..."

If you had an opening and I happened to be a phenomenal player and was named Jethro, would I be considered?

IA: (without laughing) "I would not make the decision on my own ... I don't make all the decisions, like which hotel to stay in, playing certain places, etc. The band is somewhat of a democracy. If you were trying out, you would be put up for a vote, and your performance and personality would be considered in the decision, and not your name. Although, if your name was Jethro, it would not enhance your chances." (slight chuckle)

If you were going to interview yourself, what would be the most important, or your favorite, question to ask?

IA: "If I was gay. No one ever asks me that. That was the first question I was asked on a tour to Australia several years ago. No one's asked it since. I don't know if some people have their minds made up that I am gay, or if they think I am not. I don't know. Although I'm married and have children, I've never explored ... There are certain female characteristics that are good that I appreciate. The answer is no, but I don't know for sure."

In your opinion, what have been the most significant personnel changes in Jethro Tull, and why?

IA: "There have probably been about twenty-two personnel changes. Most were of the fine musicians caliber we've had that have been in a state of transition, or were wandering in and out ... as opposed to being asked to leave."

Do you think there is less marijuana smoking at today's concerts than in the late '70s in the U.S.A?

IA: "Yes. I don't like it at my concerts. I've never liked the smell of marijuana smoke. I use my full lung capacity in concert, and I don't appreciate second-hand smoke—whether it's cigarette smoke or marijuana. I've never liked people lighting up joints at our shows. We've done our best to curtail it, but ... there's not a whole lot you can do."

I have been to a few seminars in my time (which were) put on by well-meaning speakers, on the subject of rock music from a Christian's perspective. They have often painted the song and album *Aqua Lung* as being an anti-Christ message. In response to this, what is the real scoop on that song?

IA: "I have never heard someone say this to me. In correspondence over the years, even from people involved in the Christian faith professionally, they have always said they appreciated the lyrics to the songs on that album. Two or three songs on the album are written from my perspective as an angry young man, crying out against the politics of organized religion. I've always been angered and upset by the politics involved and the practices which seem to be 180 degrees diametrically opposed to the teachings of Christianity. There are those that ... you can turn on the news any day and hear about people who give the good name of Jesus Christ a bad taste. The songs on that album are not written as anti-Christ."

I have a list of six bands that I'd like you to comment on the music and live performances of.

Yes:

IA: "Great band. We toured with them in the early years. I appreciate their tight playing and songwriting ... certainly one of those bands that have a place in the history of rock 'n' roll. I've been trying to buy their latest album for a while now. Just today I was in a record shop, and even went over to the 'Yelp' section and had the new Yes album, but then I looked at the queue and decided, 'I'm going to be standing right here for the next twenty minutes,' and I said, 'Forget it!' I'll have to try to get this album again next time."

Kansas:

IA: "I wish I had something to say about Kansas. They were playing about the same time as we were in the States oftentimes, and I have just never had the chance to see them. I hadn't heard their music until last year. An acquaintance was talking to us about signing a contract with their company, and they sent me an album of theirs performing their classics with an orchestra."

Emerson, Lake, and Palmer:

IA: "'The Elps,' as I call them. I like their brashness; their bombastic sounds really get in your face. I'm quite fond of them. I never had a chance to see them until a few years ago when we toured together. Seeing them for thirty or forty nights on that tour was quite enjoyable."

Rush:

IA: "I don't know their music. I haven't heard it."

Led Zeppelin:

IA: "As stated before, we toured with them as a supporting act ... At one time or another I purchased all their albums. They took some stuff that wasn't quite original, but what they did with it was very special."

Metallica:

IA: "They sort of re-invented the wheel in the mid-'80s, I think it was. They took elements that were well exploited by other bands in the realm of heavy metal, and made their own sound with it. Now they've been around for fifteen or more years, which is almost half the time that Jethro Tull has been around, so if they keep going for another fifteen years, they'll guarantee a spot in the annals of rock 'n' roll."

I don't mean to pry with the next question, and I'd understand if you were reluctant to answer ... I meant to look up to see who handled your songwriting and publishing, whether it was BMI or ASCAP or some other organization, but Jethro Tull has a few songs that are staples on classic rock radio. What is your quarterly songwriting royalty payment like?

IA: "Quarterly? We get paid twice a year. My songwriting royalties are between half a million and a million. I think anyone that's selling a million albums in a year will see about a million dollars in songwriting royalties. Bands like Led Zeppelin and Pink Floyd, who I think are selling two to three million albums from their catalog every year, are certainly people who don't have to work. They could go fishing or whatever. Other motivations besides having to work to survive are what motivate them to keep making music."

What do you think of Jesus Christ?

IA: "Well, He certainly walked the earth. I do not believe some of the claims people have about Him. Should I say, 'He hasn't proved Himself to me?' Maybe if He appeared to me and showed me that He was a deity, then I would think differently ... if I had that opportunity, and, uh, if that should, from some miraculous way, come about, I'm pretty sure I would return to the here and now and I wouldn't tell a soul about it. (laughs) I would keep it to myself."

What do you think of His claims to be "the Way, The Truth, and The Life; no one comes to the Father but by Me?"

IA: "Um, well, I'm not sure, you see ... that ... you say those are His claims. I can't really, honestly, be sure that they ... they would've been. I rather doubt ... I kinda doubt that He would've really said that. I think there's some, you know, things will have been attributed to Jesus that were probably not really His words or, in some cases, maybe His actions. I think that, substantially, we probably believe in a lot of it, but I rather doubt that He would have said that. It sounds a little pompous to me.

"I think that, uh, the message of Jesus is a message of ... uh, the Son of God in a more generalized sense, I think. I don't really ... I would doubt that Jesus would really have expected us to believe in Him as being someone unique and so special as some people ascribe ... Jesus as having that, uh, beyond human quality. I think the whole value of Jesus in one of the world's most important prophetic religions is to show us that, through a regular human, flesh-and-blood guy, you can attain the full knowledge of the divine—of the absolute. Therein lies the attraction. Not to elevate Jesus to something that is beyond human or superhuman. I think that then it loses the plot. It loses the vitality of the message.

"So, um, I've been a little wary of something as, um ... uh, as grandiose as saying, 'Hey! You can only achieve this through me.' That would seem to me not to be, uh ... not to be appropriate, because I believe that you could achieve the same things through the messages and the appropriate following of ... uh ... of Islam or even Hinduism; which, although with its vast number of gods, still, at the back of it, there is a monotheistic belief. There is a single deity, a single creator behind Hinduism and, uh, the gods you encounter along the way are just that—just, uh, that's just the subcontinent's way of mixing up religion with a little bit of Walt Disney, you know? It's just colorful; it's a little fun. It helps some people channel their thoughts, but at the back of it all is a single creator and, um I ... I, I'm afraid I can't accept the idea that Jesus Christ is, "I'm the only way; you can only find your way to the truth and the absolutes through Me." I think it's more like the idea of, uh, forgiving through the teaching, through the example. That—that is the important thing. I'm afraid I can't really believe that Jesus really did say that. I kinda doubt it."

What would you base your criticism of that, uh, that claim on?

IA: "Well, you know, things must have been ... um, if you take the way things evolve—even from somebody in show business, you know, who says a certain thing or does a certain thing ... You know, Ozzy Osbourne was reputed to have bitten the head off a pigeon or rat or some such animal as I recall, back in the early '70s. You know, these things become, uh ... um, you know, they become folklore—they become legend sometimes, even though it is basically just a load of rubbish. I mean, it's just a) either a PR man has dreamt it up, um, but those in concern don't do anything to quash the rumors, because it's kind of good for publicity—it's good for the image, it adds a little uncertainty, a little drama, a little excitement, and, you know, these things happen. And I suspect that probably these things have happened in terms of some aspects of the development of the world's great religions. There's been a certain amount of real stuff happen and a certain amount of stuff got invented and embellished along the way, and I'd be very, very surprised ... I mean, I would be totally amazed if this had not happened in the evolution of Christianity. And I think we have to be on guard, we have to be aware of that. And be a little bit cautious before we believe every single thing we read about Jesus Christ and the evolution of the Christian religion. There has just got to be a little bit of exaggeration in there somewhere—a little bit of creative PR exercising going on, a little bit of a spin, you know, a little bit of spin doctoring going on. (laughs) It must have happened.

"And that's part of the thing you have to wrestle with when you follow and go into any religion. You've got to be able to accept and steer your way through some of the maze. Some of it, you know, will be a little contradictory, a little difficult to deal with. Some of it will probably make you a little angry or concerned that maybe you're being thrown a line here, and that's not quite believable. I see no possibility that the Christian religion has not suffered from a little spin doctoring along the way. And so, you know, we have to be careful. And underlying all of that is a pragmatic message, which is fundamentally good, is fundamentally common sense, and is fundamentally inspiring. That's the good thing about Christianity. But I don't believe everything is good about Christianity or any other world religion. I believe our job as individual crusaders seeking any kind of spiritual truth is to sift through things and be prepared to listen to other people, listen to their advice, listen to their thoughts, their criticism, their beliefs, and we have to make up our own minds—what we choose to believe, what we choose to take as being the things that are precious and relevant to us. We have to be prepared to discard some things that we ultimately decide we can't go along with. I don't think that makes us bad people. I don't think that will make us rejected at the doors of the kingdom of heaven. (laughs) I think that we have a lifetime ahead of us to figure that out. And we will not be penalized by a God in heaven or in any other environment, just because maybe we fell under a bus before we actually, finally managed to figure it all out. I think we will not be penalized for taking our time to weigh things out. And I really do have this belief that we should all be making that effort to figure things out for us. And we use the help that is at hand. Sometimes that help will come through organized religion; sometimes it'll come from a member of your family, or somebody you meet in the street. It'll come from all sorts of different places throughout your life, but you use all those as little clues, and you put the pieces of the jigsaw puzzle together, and maybe one day you figure it out and decide what you really do believe in and where you're going to go with the rest of your life. But some people may figure that out when they're ten years old; some maybe figure it out when they're fifty years old. Some don't figure it out at all. But, I don't believe you're penalized just because you're a little slower than somebody else. I think that would be ... that's not the God I believe in. You know, He will not reject me, you, or anybody else just because we haven't quite got it figured out. Maybe we still harbor some elements of doubt. I don't think that's going to be, uh ... that doesn't mean we're in the exclusion zone.

"And with those words of encouragement and solace, (laughs) and hope, I must leave you, because I must get on to the next thing that I have to do."

[Never before published, conducted in '01]

"Jesus is there
no matter
what the
(expletive)
goes down."

—Jesse Camp

{JESSE CAMP

20 J

photo by Mark Weiss

Jesse Camp is a real sweetheart. If you have ever caught him VJ-ing on MTV, your first impression may have been "space cadet!" But in conversation (here with Jamie Lee Rake), he's the friendly kind of guy who immediately warms up to you and wants to be your bud. And you can't help but want to be his. He brings that out in you.

Camp recently got back to his first love—making catchy hard rock in a glam/punk/metal mode—with the release of his first album, Jesse & the 8th Street Kidz. *Before embarking on his first international tour, Camp did the "day of interviews" routine at his label's New York City office and deigned to go through the battery of questions for HM, which found him in the same kind of open, amiable, sometimes surprising, thoughtful mood that has endeared him to plenty of MTV viewers.*

You've been doing this rock 'n' roll thing for how long, Jesse?

JC: "My whole life, man!"

For how long have you been in bands?

JC: "Since I's a little kid, you know. My first bands, you know, were in elementary school, then in middle school. Then in high school, the band we had going then was a band called Easy Action. You know, I've always been a hyper kid, and music's always been my outlet in one way or another."

You had that band's name from the Alice Cooper record of the same name?

JC: "Yeah, that Alice Cooper record!"

What's the story behind your MTV VJ-hood?

JC: "It was an unexpected thing in my life. I'd been in high school (expletive) around with my band, kinda moved to California and doing ... and kind of hanging around all over the place. I had been squatting in New York and stuff, and they had this, uh ... You know, I was staying, me and my friend Carson were staying at the NYU dorms with these girls, and they were actress girls, and one day they were like, 'We're going down to MTV for this audition.' And we're, like, 'What?!' and they're, like, 'Yeah!' And so, we're, like, 'Can we come along?,' and they're, like, 'Sure!' And so, (expletive) man, gosh, one thing led to another, and I was auditioning for it, and it was just a very lucky break in my life. And it opened up a lot of doors for my music."

How did the hook-up with Hollywood Records come about?

JC: "Well, I had been jamming with this band called The Dogs D'Amor, and they're in various members, and a lot of dudes kind of used to be just around L.A. and stuff. My manager knew a lot of these kind of, like, old rocker dudes, and so he'd hang out with Steve Jones (The Sex Pistols), and just, like, a bunch of old rockers. We wrote a lot of songs, and our manager shopped them around to a bunch of different labels. And we decided to go with Hollywood Records because they were into the music aspect of it much more than the personalities. Being on MTV is great, but in a lot of ways, it's not what I want to do with my life, and how exactly I wasn't always allowed to be myself on it, whereas when I'm doing the show (concert). This is me, and this is the vibe we're doing. This is 1,000 percent Jesse Camp."

How would you describe Jesse & The 8th Street Kidz?

JC: "If anyone asks what kind of music we play, I'd just say it's our music. There's no better title or classification. Sure, a lot of my favorite bands are Hanoi Rocks, Kiss, Aerosmith, The Dead Boys, The New York Dolls, or Motorhead. Those bands definitely influenced us, but I never want to be the kind of guy who says, 'If you like Aerosmith, If you like Guns N' Roses, you'll like us.' We're definitely on our own trip, and lyrically I write the things that come out of my head, and out of my mind, and out of my soul. So it's definitely a unique trip.

"I don't think there has ever been music made like the music we make, you know. I think every band's on their own individual trip, as long as they're making the music that is in their souls, and they're not, like, double-thinking, 'Well, if I make this kind of music, we'll get this kind of kid at a show.' You just got to do what makes you happy, and all I can describe (our music) as is our music. But it's definitely, (expletive), yeah ... we wear the hard rock banner on our sleeves with pride."

Are you going to be touring behind the album?

JC: "Are you kidding?! We're going to be touring for the rest of our lives! We're playing everywhere in America. Then we'll go over to Europe and Japan."

What's the reaction been to you overseas?

JC: "The record's gotten a good buzz in Japan and stuff. That's great, too, because a lot of people over there, they just know us solely for our music. At the end of the day, it's like, yeah, I like to fool around and have fun on TV, but when you come to our show, that's what we're about. We're just a good rock 'n' roll band playing for people who love rock 'n' roll. I think that relates everywhere, you know what I mean?"

What more do you want to do after this?

JC: "We just got so many more songs we want to get out. We keep writing songs and songs and songs, and I guess my ultimate goal in life is to write a musical masterpiece one day. I want to play as many concerts as we can to as many people as we can. Also, in my lyrics, I write lyrics that describe a lot of the problems and (expletive) that I've been through, in a way to kind of help other people through similar problems and stuff. So, as long as I can help other people with my lyrics ...

"And all it is that I want is to have a (expletive) good time, (expletive) as many girls as I can, do as many ... well ... I just want to enjoy life to the fullest."

Your bio says rock 'n' roll has been your salvation. In what way?

JC: "Well, in a lot of ways. I grew up in a situation that was much more conservative. And I grew up with a lot of people that were at odds with me. I was always (expletive) different than the people in my life, and what I mean by that is that at school the teachers would always kind of look at you funny. And you'd go home, and my parents loved me the way they can, but they also gave me a lot of (expletive). Growing up that way, it's very easy to fall into the trap of, 'Maybe all these other people in my life are right, and maybe I'm wrong.'

"It's like, no, at the end of the day, I had to realize that, '(expletive) no, dude, I'm a rock 'n' roller. I'm gonna be a rock 'n' roller, and if anyone has a problem with that, they can (expletive). I'm just gonna make the kind of music I love.' It's sorta like, rock 'n' roll gave me a way out of that small town. It gave me a way out of the small-minded thinking of a lot of my teachers and parents."

I wanted to ask you about one song on the album, specifically "My Little Saviour." What's that about?

JC: "Well, I wrote that when I was sixteen, and I used to kind of trip out, road trip with this girl, Lee Ann, and we always used to Greyhound up and down the coast a whole lot, and—that's kind of how "Sloppy Kisses" came about, too—but basically that song's about having that one person in your life that you love and sticks by you. You know, a lot of my life I've lived fiercely independent, because I never had that salvation, and I realized that you can find that love and that there are other people that understand you and are going to be there for you unconditionally. It's about unconditional love that you have for that other person. Once you find your soul mate, the world can fling whatever it wants at you, and you'll always make it out as long as you have someone that loves you and has your back and you have their back. That's what that song's about."

I don't know if (the publicist) told you, but this interview is for a Christian hard music magazine, *HM* ...

JC: "Sure."

And that would, of course, mean that Jesus is our Savior. So, what's your opinion of Him? Have you read much about Him?

JC: "Jesus? I (expletive) gotta say I definitely believe in karma, and I believe that what comes around goes around and that, in life, it's like, you get what you give. And, you know, it's about healing. I think that there are lot of times when, it's like, you grow up tough, and you grow up the hard way. And maybe you have parents that are doing a lot of (expletive) skeezy (expletive). You know it's wrong, but you kind of fall into the same cycle. I think there are a lot of parents out there who give their kids a lot of hell because they're still in their old cycle, so they bring up a lot of kids with a lot of emptiness and a lot of wounds in them. It's very easy to kind of try to fill those wounds with a lot of self-destructive behavior. But the thing in life is, you gotta (expletive), you gotta break that cycle and fill that emptiness with the love of other people who really love you for you."

And we would say that Jesus can love you like anybody else ever.

JC: "I think of Jesus when I think of someone having your back. (Expletive) Jesus is there no matter what the (expletive) goes down. It's never too late that He'll always have your back at the end of the world. That (expletive) faith is the most important thing. If you have faith in God, then you have faith in yourself because God is never gonna let you down. He's gonna put you through some hard (expletive), but He always has your back at the end of the day as long as you got your own back."

What would you think, then, of C.S. Lewis's statement that Jesus has to be either a liar, lunatic, or Lord in order to call Himself Savior?

JC: "I'll have to say ... man, I don't even think you have to make things so complicated. I just look at Jesus as a good buddy, you know. I try to make everyone I meet into a good buddy, you know."

I get that vibe from you.

JC: "It's sorta like, I mean, Jamie, it's sorta like everyone in life is on their own trip. And anger is a bad thing because I don't believe anyone is evil. I just believe that people have been misled and bad situations and don't know how to react to them. It's sort of like ... man, I did some (expletive) things 'cause I didn't know how to deal with it, and it was all new. Life's full of tests and tribulations. Even though other people are being tested, we all interact with one another, so we have to be courteous of the (expletive) other people are going through. I think at the end of the day, everyone's your brother, even if they aren't feeling that way at the time.

"Sort of like when someone's drunk, dude. They're gonna say some (expletive) they don't really mean in the morning. But, it's like, they're drunk, and you have to take care of them. You know, you still better give him a ride home.

"But, I hope this record definitely is very inspirational. I mean, I'm definitely a very spiritual person, and in my lyrics, especially songs like 'Summertime Squatters' and 'Slow Down,' a lot of my battles that I've had with my faith and a lot of my insecurities and a lot of my tests and tribulations that I think God's put me through, I try to speak about so that other people can maybe identify.

"You know what it's like when a butterfly's kind of going through its cocoon, and he changes? Well, I've had a lot of changes in my life, and I know there are a lot of kids that are kind of going through that too. In my lyrics, I try to explain the changes, so maybe they don't feel alone. And I'm glad to have been on MTV because there are really a lot of heavy metal fans and a lot of kids out there that sort of feel very alone and feel like they don't have anyone to relate to on TV because everyone's so prim and proper and clean cut. It's like, yeah, I'm different, you know, sometimes, but (expletive) if I don't like having a good time as much as everyone else. At the end of the day, it's like, I'm still a (expletive) real kid. I think maybe I was able to be there for a lot of other kids who come from conservative backgrounds and stuff like that, because, you know, sometimes you need other people to believe in.

"I think that spirituality gets a bum rap because a lot of people try to bring kids up ... I think believing in God and loving God has nothing to do with going to this big, old, strict Texas church. I think it has to do with believing in and loving with God, and I think that a dude that (expletive) takes care of people and gives them the shirt off their back in real life, that counts so much more than a dude that who goes to church every day but is a (expletive) on the street."

I would say that maybe you need some of each, Jess.

JC: "I definitely, though, believe that you need—I agree with that. I think that if you love God, then that's gonna come through what you're doing, but I'm trying to say that maybe sometimes people mix spirituality with, um ... some of ... do you know what I'm trying to say? I think sometimes people mix up being a good person, if they know a lot of people ... What I'm trying to say is that your relationship in spirit with God is something you're going to give naturally on your own, and it's ... that being a good person is something you should do in and out of church."

Exactly, exactly, and we believe Jesus is the best example of that.

JC: "Yeah! And I think that church is, is a very good place where you can always kind of get your bearings back. It's very much Jesus' home.

"I know what it's like to be a (expletive) street kid, to have nothing to (expletive) eat, to have no home. And I got to say that there are so many people that (expletive) supported me, helped me out, brought me into their homes during my hard times and my search. There have been times when I wanted to throw in the (expletive), 'What the (expletive) is this life for?' And it's just that I've had so many people then that have been (expletive) like, 'No, kid, this is what you live for,' and it helped me out through those hard times. I think that at the end of the day, it's God that's there for all of us, and we just gotta (expletive) do our best to be the good Christian that He wants us to be."

You'd call yourself a Christian then?

JC: "Yeah."

Okay, I'll be praying for you, man.

JC: "Jamie, I also wanted to say that having this talk made me remember a lot of (expletive), and I wanted to thank you for that."

You're welcome.

[Originally printed in May/June Issue '00 #83]

THOUGHTS ON
EVANGELISM

One of the central elements to Jesus' messages on evangelism (if we can single out some of His teachings and put a broad label on this aspect) is the concept of planting seeds. One plants, another waters, another harvests. God provides the increase and growth. All of us are on a journey of discovering, knowing, and growing with God. None of us have arrived, and therefore none of us should take pride in our level of development. We are God's plants, and we mustn't forget—He has the ability and even somewhat of a penchant for "pruning." This is often not pleasant. Oh, were it so that we could learn some of our lessons without pain!

If we rejoice in watching a seed grow—and we should—we ought to also remember that our growth happens at different speeds. You do not see a gardener tugging at his plants, willing them to stretch their stalks and leaves, do you? In a similar fashion, our misguided efforts to help a person "grow faster in their faith" could more accurately be seen as meddling, and that from the most important perspective in the universe—God's.

One piece of advice I'd like to give is: Watch your elders. Look for wisdom. Go visit an elderly Sunday school class. If a dispute about a doctrine or extra-biblical controversy breaks out, look around the room. Invariably, there are those one or two individuals who have a calm peace in the midst of an argument. Others may even get perturbed that these people don't take one side or the other in the debate. Learn from these people. They have realized that only a few things that are important in this life—and being right about a certain doctrine or truth is often not one of them. What may seem like a life or death matter, from God's perspective, may be very shallow and short-term. The "life or death" matters that we face in our lives prob-ably come in obvious ways, like adrenaline-charged moments where we actually are pulling another human being out of a burning automobile. If we relax and trust that God will lead us via the teaching and wisdom found in His Word, as well as the character-forming that His Spirit does in our lives, then we can quickly respond in obedience when necessary, and show off the peace that passes understanding in the majority of the other times.

In the "grand scheme" of things, God has placed the job of evangelism in our hands. Matthew 28:18-20, considered the "Great Commission," teaches the followers (or "disciples") of Jesus to go and make more followers of Him. The context of this oft-quoted Scripture (and others like it) is climactic. Jesus has risen from the dead, shown Himself to His disciples, and, prior to ascending to heaven from the Mount of Olives, He reinforces His teachings, emphasizing what's important, and then He physically leaves His followers to begin a new era in the kingdom of God. In this context, these teachings are surely some of His most important. One can safely conclude that making disciples (or "winning souls" or "evangelism") is very high on the priority list of duties for God's people.

Why He left the job to His followers is a good question. Certainly God could cover the circumference of the earth with a thin layer of clouds and impose a high definition image of Himself and deliver a message to everyone on earth that could be heard in every language and dialect. He's been known to show signs of Himself in the distant past, so why not get the "job" done quickly with a celestial press conference? I do not know the answer to this question any more than I know why God has chosen to limit Himself, many times, by responding to prayer rather than simply imposing His will. (Maybe watching the film *Bruce Almighty*, and others like it, over and over again will give me some insight on this one.) I believe it is simply a fact of God's design and order that we must deal with accordingly if we desire to be obedient to His will. While it is a mysterious plan—winning the world for Christ—it is a beautiful one. We are quite figuratively Christ's hands and feet. We are the ones that carry on His work on earth. If we are to stay true to His Word, we cannot neglect the poor, the hungry, and the needy. Besides the obvious results of practical love (a listening and attentive audience), it is also quite literally a sign for the intelligent but skeptical non-believer to see Christ at work on earth. Loving and caring for those around us is an undeniable sign to the world that God is at work. And the beautiful part of that is it cannot be done with the motive of trying to convert someone that you think is somehow below you or not as good as you. More than likely, in order for it to have a huge impact, it must be real. It must be done in love. Love is unconditional. Love gives a drink to a thirsty soul, period—not holding the cup out of their reach until they profess faith in Christ. Love must risk rejection and, if it comes, not respond in anger or out of hurt.

The good news is that, while evangelism tends to be work—living, speaking, listening, serving, writing, creating, loving, doing—the results of conversion are indeed a work of God and a miracle. In the same way that a healing or a deliverance/exorcism requires God to "show up and do His stuff," so does evangelism. Sometimes we seem to forget this fact and try to do the converting ourselves. However, knowing that conversion is an act of God can also take the pressure off of our shoulders. Certainly Christ (and even His followers, Peter, Stephen, Philip, and especially Paul) modeled bold, aggressive, and compelling speech, but coercion was never used. Jesus used the Old Testament prophets, the Law, and the Psalms to convince those around Him after the resurrection that He was the fulfillment of God's plan of redemption. Peter used bold and fresh current events in his pleas to his audience (and won three thousand converts after one speech). Philip reasoned with an Ethiopian official out of the book of Isaiah. Paul argued in Athens with the proficiency of a lawyer in court. We will do well to be inspired by these men of God and strive to add to their accomplishments; however, the end results are always God's doing. If God's Holy Spirit does not show up to give the living, breathing, and willing person a new heart of flesh to replace their heart of stone, all our words are just that—words.

Each reader, each person in this world, is valuable to God. This is exemplified in the words Christ chose to identify those who did not believe in Him and His message. He didn't call those who doubted "losers," nor those who chose to not believe in Him "lowlifes." He labeled such people as "lost." Lost connotes value. If you misplace something that's worthless, you probably don't even look for it, much less call it lost. But if you lose something valuable, you search for that lost item until it is found. People are important. May this book—and more importantly the lives we live—help many to be "found" by their Creator.